Managing a guide for older people

Edited by
Yvonne Gallacher & Jim Gray

AGE
Concern

Bulk orders

Age Concern England is pleased to offer customised editions of all its titles to UK companies, institutions or other organisations wishing to make a bulk purchase. For further information, please contact the Publishing Department at the address on this page. Tel: 020 8765 7200. Fax: 020 8765 7211. Email: books@ace.org.uk

© 2002 Yvonne Gallacher and Jim Gray

Published by Age Concern England
1268 London Road
London SW16 4ER

First published 2002

Edited by Yvonne Gallacher and Jim Gray
Production   Ro Lyon and Vinnette Marshall
Design and typesetting   GreenGate Publishing Services
Printed in Great Britain by Bell & Bain Ltd, Glasgow

A catalogue record for this book is available from the British Library.

ISBN 0-86242-236-1

This book is based on an original concept by Rex Mottershead.

Contents

About the editors

Yvonne Gallacher has been Chief Executive of Money Advice Scotland since April 1997. She has 14 years' experience in consumer credit and money advice. She comes from a local authority Trading Standards background, having been employed in the public sector for 22 years in total, including 12 years within the police service. An advocate of standards, qualifications and accreditation, Yvonne has been involved in developing the standards/qualifications in advice, and is Company Secretary and Director of the Lead Body, which developed the occupational standards in advice. She has been a lecturer at North Glasgow College delivering the Higher National Certificate (HNC) in Welfare Rights and Money Advice, which she developed in conjunction with two colleagues and college staff.

Yvonne has co-authored a technical handbook *A Guide to Money Advice in Scotland* and other information and factsheets about money advice. She is a member of various organisations, including: the Scottish Consumer Council; the Financial Services Authority's Independent Consumer Panel and Consumer Education Forum; the Scottish Qualifications Authority Care Advisory Group; and the UK Money Advice Trust Advisory Committee.

Jim Gray is currently Partnership Manager of Drumchapel Social Inclusion Partnership, which is part of the Glasgow Alliance regeneration agency. He was previously Senior Solicitor and Manager of Drumchapel Law and Money Advice Centre, and prior to that post was a Welfare Rights Development Officer with the former Strathclyde Regional Council.

Jim is co-author, with Yvonne, of *A Guide to Money Advice in Scotland* and has also written several other advice publications. He co-designed the HNC in Welfare Rights and Money Advice and has been a visiting lecturer at North Glasgow College and Glasgow University.

Acknowledgements

The editors would like to acknowledge the assistance of the following individuals who have contributed to the production of this book:

Jemiel Benison for writing Chapter 5
Sophie Brookes for writing Chapters 6 and 7
Liz Willis for writing Chapter 4
Meg van Rooyen for commenting on Chapters 6 and 7

Yvonne Gallacher also wishes to acknowledge Jim Gray's contribution in writing Chapters 1–3, and for the introduction to the book.

The editors would also like to thank all of the reviewers, including:

Lorna Easterbrook
Jeremy Fennell
Alison Hopkins
Jenny Jenkins
Janet Wilson

Introduction

The aim of this book

This book aims to equip you with the basic information needed to help you deal with financial problems, whether you yourself are in debt or whether you are advising an older person who is in debt. It does not cover financial advice on pensions and investments. It does not offer any guidance on the financial planning required by people seeking to protect assets. Similarly, it looks at taxation as it adds to liabilities, but not in respect of tax planning. Essentially this book is a guide to the action that older people can take when experiencing financial hardship. It concentrates primarily on debt and on how to manage on a limited income.

In a book on this subject some of the terms used are inevitably highly technical and may seem to be 'jargon'. It is important, however, to know what these mean since they are terms that you will encounter when dealing with debt. **Technical terms are therefore italicised in the text and explained in a glossary at the back of the book.** The law quoted throughout is that of England and Wales as at 30 November 2001.

Older people and debt

Few older people have significant savings or investments to help finance a comfortable retirement. A 1999 survey found that, excluding the value of their home, 57 per cent of older people had less than £3,000 in savings or investments and only 8 per cent had over £30,000 (*With Respect to Old Age: Long-term care – rights and responsibilities – Cmnd 4192*).

Many people experience financial problems in retirement. Despite the general rise in living standards enjoyed by the population generally, the survey showed that the average weekly income of individuals between the ages of 55 and 69 remained below £100.

A book published 25 years ago about the financial problems of older people would have concentrated almost entirely on State benefits. In 1979, 55 per cent of pensioners relied on means-tested benefits. This figure has fallen, mainly because of the State Earnings-Related Pension Scheme (SERPS) and occupational and personal pensions, to the extent that by 1995 only 36 per cent of pensioners relied on the means-tested benefit Income Support.

Having grown up in times of depression and then the Second World War, the older generation believed in traditional values of thrift and 'paying their way'. Even by 1989, by which time 60 per cent of the population were using credit, the Office of Fair Trading study *Overindebtedness* found that 50 per cent of those aged over 65 would not use credit as a matter of principle. Reasons given included: 'if we want anything we save up for it' and 'if we can't afford it we do without it'.

Although these attitudes continue to affect the use of personal credit by older people, other factors have contributed to an increase in credit. These include: the increase in home ownership and changing use of mortgages (eg capital release); higher expectations in retirement; the longer time spent in retirement by many people; and the issue of having to pay for care.

Debt has also increased over the last 25 years. A Policy Studies Institute report in 1992, *Credit and Debt*, found that:

- 1 in 5 households was in arrears
- 1 in 8 households had problem debts
- 1 in 12 households had 'unmanaged debts'

Inability to pay was caused by a number of factors, including: unemployment; decreased income; illness and disability; relationship breakdown; and family crisis (eg bereavement).

Many people acquire debts because they need to use credit as their only method of buying essential household goods – such as furniture and clothing – as their income is insufficient to budget for replacements. More than 14 million people now live on less than half the national average income (Child Poverty Action Group's *Poverty Facts and Figures*). More than 20 per cent of all households do not have a bank account or access to credit from banks and major financial institutions (HM Treasury Policy Action Team Report 14/1999). Many people begin as 'consumer debtors' but over time become caught in a poverty trap in which they cannot hope to meet their commitments even with *rescheduling* of debts. Changes in circumstances, such as separation, illness or retirement, can often cause people to get into debt.

Whatever the cause of the debts, these statistics illustrate just how widespread financial problems are in our society. Financial problems can in turn lead to other difficulties. People of all ages, but older people in particular, may experience feelings of guilt, shame and humiliation, in addition to the anxiety caused by lack of money and pressure from creditors to make payments. Coping with these emotions can be difficult and physical or mental health problems may ensue. Some people may already have addictions or behavioural problems. Such people will be helped by advice on dealing with money as a preliminary to obtaining assistance with the underlying problem.

However, the overwhelming majority of people with financial problems will benefit from advice about dealing with debts (often known as 'money advice') and will not need specialised counselling. Recognising and admitting that you have financial problems is a crucial first step in solving them. The first chapter of this book offers suggestions on seeking money advice and lists some relevant advice agencies and other organisations. The book also provides practical assistance in addressing your problems and will enable you to take positive steps to deal with your situation. It makes it clear when you are likely to need to seek advice, whilst outlining the steps involved in: drawing up a Personal Budget; checking that you are getting all the State benefits and other income that you are entitled to; prioritising debts and dealing with emergencies; negotiating with creditors; and dealing with the County Court and with bankruptcy.

1 Seeking money advice

Although this book can help you try to sort out your financial problems by yourself, not everyone will feel able to tackle everything themselves and some of the more legal aspects can be very complex anyway. It is important that you feel confident about the actions suggested and that you are clear in your own mind that you understand which approach fits your circumstances. At the very least it will usually be worth getting a second opinion on your circumstances.

This chapter covers:

- *Deciding whether to get advice*
- *What types of advice are available?*
- *Selecting where to go for advice*
- *Free impartial, independent and confidential advice*
- *Independent advice where you may have to pay a contribution*
- *Advice where a fee will be charged*
- *Consumer Credit Counselling Service*

Deciding whether to get advice

As we said in the introduction, recognising that you have a financial problem is a crucial first step in solving it. Many people feel a range of emotions in such circumstances – failure, humiliation, shame, depression, guilt, fear – and coping with these emotions can be difficult. It may be that the added burden of trying to negotiate with creditors is too much if you are feeling some or all of these emotions. In such cases, there is a lot to be said for getting advice from an independent, non-judgmental adviser who will be able to take some of the pressure off you. The responsibility for solving the problem remains with you but the adviser will be able to help you put your problem in perspective and help with the processes and procedures.

1

If you do feel confident about dealing with the problem yourself, or with a minimum of assistance, there are a few golden rules that you need to follow. These are:

1 Essential tools which you require are:
   - A calculator
   - Access to a computer or typewriter
   - Access to a photocopier

2 Remember to keep copies of:
   - Everything you send to creditors (send letters by recorded delivery or ask the post office for proof of posting)
   - All letters from creditors
   - A note of phone calls and the names of people you spoke to

3 Negotiating techniques:
   - Be calm and assertive; never lose your temper
   - If you are getting nowhere, ask to speak to a more senior person
   - Don't be pressurised into an agreement you cannot afford
   - Be realistic and never make promises you can't keep
   - Don't panic
   - If you are losing confidence, seek advice

Wherever you go for advice, it is essential that you:
   - understand the nature of the service available;
   - feel confident in the ability of the person advising you (ie that they are competent and independent); and
   - give them a full and accurate picture of your financial situation (advisers should not just deal with one debt but all of them).

What types of advice are available?

There is a wide variety of providers of money advice, across the public, voluntary and private sectors. The next sections are designed to help you make an informed choice when selecting who to approach for help. **(Contact addresses and telephone numbers are included in the 'Useful addresses' section at the end of the book.)**

The type of assistance available will vary according to the practice and policies of the agency you consult and where you live. Some offer advice on a self-help model – ie they talk you through what to do, either in person or over the telephone, leaving it up to you to write letters and make telephone calls to your creditors. Others will take things a stage further and will help you to construct a financial statement and help draft letters with you. Other agencies will accept you as a client (or user or customer) and will offer to draft a financial statement or letters with information that you provide, and ask you to sign a form which will authorise your creditors to deal with the adviser, and release information etc. However, in all such cases you remain in control and the adviser should not agree to anything without your consent.

Selecting where to go for advice

There are a few general rules that you should follow when selecting a provider. These are:

- How did you hear about them? Whichever sector they are in, try not to rely solely on their own publicity. Try to check out their success record independently with another source listed here.
- Don't expect miracles and treat absolute assurances with scepticism. Negotiating with creditors is not an exact science. Someone telling you hard facts, and that they'll do their best, is more likely to be reliable than empty promises.
- All agencies should have a Category D licence to provide debt counselling (issued by the Office of Fair Trading under the Consumer Credit Act 1974) unless they are exempt, or have powers under other legislation. Local authorities, for example, are exempt from licensing. Citizens Advice Bureaux and members of the Federation of Information and Advice Centres are covered by a Group licence issued by the Office of Fair Trading. If in doubt, ask the agency to confirm its position. The regulatory framework is very loose, and it is relatively easy to get a licence and set up a debt adjustment/negotiation business, provided that the applicant has

3

no convictions for dishonesty, fraud or *bankruptcy*. There is no equivalent of the stringent regime now imposed on independent financial advisers. For this reason, we go into more detail below on debt adjustment firms.

Free impartial, independent and confidential advice

Most advice agencies advertise their services widely – check at your local library or in the telephone directory for details. Access to advice agencies is by telephone or personal visit. In advance of a visit, you should check catchment areas, opening hours and whether you need to make an appointment.

1 **Age Concern** – locally and nationally Age Concern can offer information about income and benefit issues for older people. In some places this will be by telephone only; in other places it will be in person. Some Age Concern organisations and groups offer more detailed advice and in almost all other cases referral to other specialist agencies will be made. Membership of the Age Concern federation involves meeting specific quality standards and in addition many services now meet strict criteria set by the Community Legal Service for its Quality Mark standard. You can find out where your nearest local Age Concern is by phoning 0800 00 99 66 or by looking in the phone book.

2 **Citizens Advice Bureaux (CABx)** – most CABx will be able to offer free advice on debt problems, either by telephone or in person. Some CABx have specialist debt advice staff while others rely on generalist volunteers. You should check what service is available when you contact them. All CABx have to meet membership criteria set by the National Association of Citizens' Advice Bureaux and they are registered charities. As well as being free and independent, CABx are impartial, non-judgmental and have strict equal opportunities policies. You can find out where your nearest CAB is from the phone book or at your local library.

3 **National Debtline** – as the name implies, this is a telephone advice service. Advisers are all trained specialists who will talk

you through your problem. They will send you a self-help pack and/or factsheets on particular areas, such as mortgage debt. The self-help packs include examples of financial statements and letters to creditors. They will support you and give advice on how to complete a financial statement for example. There is no limit on the number of times that you can approach them for help.

4 **The Money Advice Association** – this is the umbrella organisation for money advice providers for England and Wales. It will be able to put you in touch with your nearest agency providing free independent, confidential advice. The telephone number is on page 165.

5 **Law centres** – many urban areas have law centres staffed by solicitors and paralegals (ie people trained in legal matters, but not fully qualified as lawyers). You should check whether your local one provides a service in debt cases. The service may be free – check this with them. You can find out if there is a law centre locally by looking in the phone book, asking the CAB or phoning the Law Centres Federation at the number on page 165. (See also 'Community Legal Service' below.)

6 **Local authorities** – many local authorities provide welfare rights and money advice services free to local residents. These are often located in social services departments but some may be in the housing, finance or trading standards departments.

Independent advice where you may have to pay a contribution

1 **Community Legal Service** – this is the new name for legal aid, advice and assistance for civil matters such as debt. It is being built up on the basis of the former legal aid franchising system. It now includes both solicitors in private practice, and law centres and CABx. You will have access to solicitors and/or paralegals. You may be assessed to pay a contribution towards the cost of the advice depending upon the level of your income and capital.

5

Advice where a fee will be charged

1 **Solicitors and Chartered Accountants** – solicitors may operate outside the Community Legal Service, and be prepared to advise you for an agreed fee. You may have a family solicitor whom you are used to dealing with and whom you trust. If they do debt work, and you want to use them, try to agree a fixed fee for a set amount of work. Many private solicitors now charge up to £100 per hour, and you need to be clear what you can afford.

The Law Society publishes the Solicitors Regional Directory for England and Wales, which sets out the names and addresses of local solicitors, the area of law and the type of work they do. Local libraries, advice agencies and CABx should have the directory.

Many Chartered Accountants offer a service to people with financial difficulties. Look out for ones who are Insolvency Practitioners as they are most likely to be able to help. Speak to a money adviser first as they may be able to help you contact one locally and will know about charging structures. Insolvency Practitioners are particularly useful if you are likely to be considering an Individual Voluntary Arrangement (IVA – see page 126). Again, you should check what fee is likely to be charged. Rates may be similar to those of solicitors. All solicitors, whether in Community Legal Services or not, must have indemnity insurance, and are subject to the rules of the Law Society. You therefore have redress against them for negligence. Chartered Accountants are subject to a similar regime.

2 **Debt adjustment /negotiation firms** – these are a relatively recent development. You may have seen adverts for them in the press and on television and the Internet. They are different from those firms which offer consolidated loans.

Make sure you are dealing with a firm that is only offering to reschedule your debts, and not also offering you a loan at a high interest rate. If any agency tries to persuade you to take out a loan with a particular company, don't do anything without speaking to an independent financial adviser (IFA). Money advisers of any description should not be giving advice on the best loans to take out. On the other hand, some IFAs are licensed to provide debt counselling and may be competent to do so.

Once you are satisfied that the firm is not trying to lend you money, check their charging policy. Some want an upfront fee from you for doing the initial work (financial statement and letters to creditors). Despite the adverts, no one can guarantee success, nor ensure that interest is frozen (unless in an Administration Order or an IVA – see pages 104 and 126). Be wary of anyone who says they can.

Ask yourself the following questions before agreeing to pay a fee up front to one of these companies:

- Can I afford to pay this fee?
- Could I get help elsewhere, either free or cheaper?
- What track record of success do they have (not based on their own publicity)?

Other firms will offer to help in return for a percentage of the amount you pay creditors. If they can't reach an agreement, they don't get paid. This may seem attractive at first sight because you are not having to pay an upfront fee. However, you should think carefully and check how much you have to pay over the repayment period, as it may add up to a great deal more than the upfront fee. You also need to remember that you have to pay this as well as the agreed amounts to your creditors.

Some creditors do not approve of fee-charging debt negotiation firms and refuse to deal with them. Their rationale is that you could get free advice elsewhere and that you should be paying your creditors, not the fee charger. Whilst this is debatable, it is worth checking with your creditors whether they will deal with the firm you propose to use.

Consumer Credit Counselling Service (CCCS)

This is a model of debt advice that has been imported from the USA. The CCCS is a not-for-profit organisation, self-financed by the deductions it makes from your payments (see below), rather than being part of the traditional voluntary sector. It received some initial start-up capital from the credit industry. It operates on the following model:

- Referrals are mostly made by the credit industry.
- A financial statement is produced.
- If there is a surplus (ie disposable income) for distribution among the creditors, the CCCS will set up an arrangement with them, known as a Debt Management Programme.
- The CCCS will manage the repayments, deducting an agreed fee from the amounts sent to creditors. No charge is made to you, as the creditors treat the amount deducted by the CCCS as a contribution towards your account.
- If you do not have a surplus to distribute, the CCCS cannot help you and will refer you to another agency.

If a creditor refers you to the CCCS, you still have a choice whether to use them. You can deal with the matter yourself or seek advice elsewhere. If the creditor refuses to negotiate with anyone else and the matter goes to court, you can refer to the offers made and rejected. Most creditors will recognise your right to choose.

The CCCS can be contacted on Freephone 0800 138 1111.

Key points

- Decide whether you need advice or want to deal with the problem yourself.

- Decide whether you can really afford to pay for advice given your current situation.

- Remember that if you do pay for advice this may exacerbate your problem as it will take longer to pay off your debts.

- If you do it yourself, keep copies of everything (ie phone calls, letters, etc).

- Be calm but assertive; don't be pressured into agreeing more than you can afford.

- If you go for advice, take all correspondence with you.

- Check opening times, catchment areas and appointment systems before you go.

- Be open and honest. Give the advice agency all the facts.

- Try to stick to an arrangement or explain why you have had to break it.

- If your circumstances change whilst seeking advice, let the money adviser know.

2 Understanding debt and credit

This chapter covers:

- *What is debt?*
- *Types of debt*
- *The main forms of consumer credit*
- *Regulation of consumer credit*

What is debt?

The answer to this question may seem obvious, but there are a number of ways in which credit can be obtained and likewise a range of consequences which result from default on payment. In other words – not all debts are the same; some are more serious than others.

The term 'debt' has been defined as:

- something owed such as money, goods or services; or
- the state of owing, of being under an obligation.

In this book we use the term 'debt' to describe the circumstances of the person owing money. What we are looking at in particular is the issue of problem debt where the person cannot repay the sums owed at the rate originally agreed with the creditor. In most cases, individuals will have several creditors and will be in a multiple debt situation.

'Debt' can arise from a variety of legal agreements. A contract is one example. A contract is a legally enforceable agreement; ie a Court can enforce the contract or award compensation for its breach.

Credit involves either buying something and being given time to pay for it (for example some mail order agreements), or borrowing money and paying it back later (for example a loan). The party giving the credit (the 'creditor') is providing a service (ie the use of the capital) in return for which the borrower (the 'debtor') is required to pay a price – such as the interest and other charges. Interest can be charged at a fixed rate from the beginning or the rate can vary over the period of the loan.

Always make sure that you understand the terms and conditions before taking out a loan – insist on an explanation if you are not clear.

Types of debt

Debts can be divided into those to be dealt with as a matter of high priority (priority debts) and those with lower priority. Chapter 4 explains in more detail about dividing the debts into these two categories as well as dealing with them.

Priority debts include:

- Utility debt (electricity and gas)
- Statutory debts (Income Tax, VAT, National Insurance contributions, Child Support, *Council Tax*, business rates, fines and civil penalties, social security overpayments and *Social Fund loans*)
- Mortgage or rent arrears
- Maintenance arrears
- Business debts (these may include several of the above and also debts owed to suppliers – some of these will be high priority as above).

Detailed advice on business debt will depend on the extent to which you are personally liable, on the one hand, or protected by limited liability on the other hand. Specialist advice should be obtained from one of the sources referred to in Chapter 1.

Non-priority debts are mainly forms of consumer credit.

The main forms of consumer credit

Bank lending

Banks offer a variety of credit facilities. They tend to charge competitive rates of interest on loans but restrict their lending to people who are relatively financially secure.

Forms of bank lending include:

Ordinary loans

These are usually restricted to a bank's own customers. A specific amount is borrowed for a particular purpose, over an agreed period, for example to buy a car or for home improvements. A loan agreement is drawn up. Variable rates of interest are charged. The bank may require some security, such as a second charge on your house.

Personal loans

This type of loan may also be available to people who are not customers of the bank. A fixed rate of interest is agreed when the loan is arranged. It tends to be a more expensive form of credit than an ordinary loan and is usually unsecured (ie security, such as property, is not required).

Overdrafts

Overdrafts arise where:

- the customer makes an arrangement with the bank to overdraw their account up to an agreed amount (an 'authorised overdraft'); or
- the customer draws more from their account than the available balance without any prior agreement (an 'unauthorised overdraft').

Banks will charge variable rates of interest on the amount of the overdraft. The interest rate is likely to be considerably higher if the overdraft is unauthorised. In addition, there will be bank charges. In the case of an unauthorised overdraft, the bank is likely to charge for its services, including for letters asking you to clear the overdraft. These are likely to be charged at a rate of at least £10 per letter and may be sent on a weekly basis until you either clear the debt in full or come to some agreement to pay.

In the case of an authorised overdraft, a detailed loan agreement is not required but there is generally some written evidence, such as a letter from the bank manager, setting out what has been agreed and the interest rate to be charged.

Whether or not the overdraft is authorised, banks have the right to use funds in any of the customer's accounts to repay the overdraft: effectively they have first call on this money unless another creditor attaches the accounts (ie seizes the funds in it by obtaining a Court order). This is how relatively manageable overdrafts can get out of hand if not dealt with promptly.

Mortgages and secured loans

These are available through banks and building societies, and other lenders. They always require a security for loan; ie the title deeds to the borrower's home. This gives the lender considerable power over you. Any further advance or capital release loan will also be secured against the house.

A variety of mortgages is available, including:

Repayment mortgages

In this type of mortgage, the capital borrowed is repaid over the period of the loan, along with interest on the balance outstanding at any time. In the early years of the loan, most of the repayments are used to pay the interest. This reverses nearer the period of the term and payments are mainly towards the capital.

Endowment mortgages

In endowment mortgages, all payments go towards the interest on the capital borrowed. Separate payments must be made to an insurance company for a policy, which will mature at the end of the term of the mortgage. The proceeds of the policy should be used to repay the capital outstanding on the loan. In practice, depending on how well the sums invested have generated growth in the fund, the policy may either pay out more than is required for repayment of the capital, or not pay out enough, leading to a shortfall in the amount needed to clear the loan. Endowment mortgages are becoming less popular as returns have decreased. Endowment providers have been required to provide predictions for payments, based on annual returns of 4 per cent, 6 per cent and 8 per cent, because of fears that many policies are underperforming. As with any investment product, seek independent financial advice before entering into or changing a mortgage.

Interest only mortgages

As the name implies, these involve the borrower making their own arrangements to repay the capital at the end of the loan period, for example through using the proceeds from Individual Savings Accounts (ISAs).

Pensions related mortgages

These are a variation of the interest only mortgages. In these schemes, part of the pension fund is used to repay the mortgage.

Other types of borrowing

Hire Purchase (HP)

Another type of credit is that of *Hire Purchase*, where, as the name suggests, the goods are hired. In HP contracts, the consumer obtains goods from the 'seller'. The seller is paid by the finance company (the 'lender'). The consumer becomes a 'borrower' and repays the debt to the lender. The goods continue to belong to the lender and are hired to the borrower until the final instalment under the agreement is paid. At that point the consumer may exercise an option to purchase the goods. Cars are often bought in this way. It is important to note that during the period of the hire purchase contract, the borrower has no title to the goods and must not dispose of them without the lender's permission.

If the borrower misses payments during the period of hire, the lender may be entitled to return of the goods. If less than one third of the total HP price has been paid, the creditor can repossess the goods if they are on public ground without a Court order. If at least one third of the total HP price has been paid, the creditor must apply through the Court for the goods to be returned. Specialist money advice should be sought in these circumstances (see Chapter 1).

Conditional sale

This is very similar to Hire Purchase and, like HP, gives the customer immediate possession but not ownership of the goods in return for regular instalments. Unlike HP, the goods become the purchaser's automatically once they have met the conditions in the contract – usually the payment of the last instalment.

Credit sale

This is now the most popular form of credit for purchasing household goods. The difference between credit sale and HP or conditional sale, is that in credit sale there are only two parties to the contract, the 'purchaser' (who is also a borrower) and the 'seller' (who is also a lender). An example is where a high street furniture shop sells a sofa which immediately belongs to you. Ownership of the goods immediately passes to the purchaser who repays a loan for the purchase price plus interest and other charges. If the borrower defaults, the lender cannot repossess the goods and must take the purchaser/borrower to Court to get their money back.

Catalogue buying

Home shopping is a very popular way of purchasing clothes and consumer goods. Whilst the Internet is revolutionising this market, traditional mail order catalogues still dominate. In many cases, payment is by weekly instalments, which may be collected by an agent and forwarded on to the company until the cost of the goods is paid off. The advantage of buying through a catalogue is that it is often interest free and allows you to spread payments. However, this is often reflected in the price of the goods, which may be higher than elsewhere.

Given the frequent lack of paperwork and the reliance on telephone orders and computer records, questions often come up about the catalogue companies' ability to establish the validity of their contract. This can give rise to disputes about the extent of a debt in the event of the customer allegedly defaulting and being pursued in the courts. It is important to keep records and copies of any paperwork or payments. Many catalogue debts may even be completely unenforceable if the customer has not signed any written agreement. Specialist money advice (see Chapter 1) should be sought if you are disputing a catalogue debt.

Credit cards

A credit card allows the holder to pay for goods or services or to obtain a cash advance by using a plastic card. The credit card company imposes a limit on the total amount of credit that can be obtained on a card. The main cardholder can also nominate other people, such as a spouse, to use a card on the account, although the main cardholder will still be liable for any purchases.

The main types of credit card are:

Bank and building society credit cards (eg MasterCard and Access)

The holder is given a personal credit limit. You can use the card to buy goods and services, or obtain a cash advance, wherever the card is accepted. There is sometimes an annual fee charged for using the service.

Shops, restaurants and other places that accept the cards send details of a purchase to the credit card company. The company pays them. You, as the cardholder, receive a statement each month showing how much you have spent. A minimum repayment – for example 5 per cent or £5 – is normally required each month. If you clear the account by a stipulated date, you are not charged any interest at all. In other cases, you will be charged interest at an agreed rate on the outstanding balance. If a payment is not made, additional administration/default fees are charged.

Debit cards (eg Visa, Switch)

A debit card is not at all like a credit card; it is more like a cheque. When you use a debit card the amount is paid straightaway from your bank account.

Charge cards (eg American Express)

These are similar to bank credit cards. The main difference is that the total balance owing must be paid in full each month.

Store cards

Many department stores or garages, for example, offer credit cards to customers for use exclusively in their own shops. They usually charge high interest rates. There are many varieties; some are debit cards.

Shop budget accounts

In many large stores you can open an account by signing an agreement or joining a scheme which then allows you to spend up to an agreed limit. This limit depends on the monthly payment that you make – for example £20 per month may give a limit of £500. Regardless of how much you spend within that limit, your monthly repayments stay the same. Interest will be charged on the amount owing at the end of each month.

Insurance policy loans

This kind of loan can be obtained from insurance companies based upon the value of an insurance policy held with them. This may be a cheap form of loan if, for example, you have an endowment policy due to mature and the company lends on a percentage of its maturity value. However, if the policy is in respect of a mortgage, payments must still be made and, if they aren't, the policy may not pay out the amount required to cover the mortgage.

In some cases it is possible to 'roll up' the interest on the loan. This means that, rather than you having to pay interest on the loan on a regular basis, the unpaid interest accrues (ie accumulates) over the period between the loan being made and your policy maturing. When the policy matures, the company will use the proceeds to clear the loan and interest and pay you the balance.

This generally offers a better deal than early surrender of the insurance policy but you should seek independent financial advice before acting.

Credit unions

Credit unions are run by their own members and encourage regular saving and offers loan facilities. Interest is charged at only 1 per cent per month on an outstanding loan. Credit unions are an attractive form of self-help, which can also open up sources of credit to individuals who have no other means of obtaining it. You can find out whether there is a credit union in your area by contacting the Association of British Credit Unions Ltd at the address on page 162 or the Financial Services Authority at the address on page 164.

Regulation of consumer credit

The cost of different forms of credit can vary greatly. In general, the lower your income, the more you will have to pay for credit. Store cards and finance companies tend to be amongst the more expensive sources of credit (finance companies are those companies that deal with credit sale, Hire Purchase and conditional sale).

Most consumer credit is regulated by the *Consumer Credit Act* 1974 (CCA) which aims to protect consumers by:

- regulating the formation and enforcement of credit agreements;
- creating a licensing system applicable to all persons involved in consumer credit, administered by the Director General of Fair Trading; and
- achieving a degree of transparency in lending, for example showing clearly the true annual rate of charge for credit (*annual percentage rate* – see page 20).

The CCA defines 'credit' as including any 'cash loan or other form of financial accommodation'.

Regulated agreements

The CCA applies to all regulated agreements. A regulated agreement is defined as 'an agreement by which the creditor provides the individual with credit not exceeding £25,000' (unless it is specifically exempted) or not exceeding £15,000 for loans taken out before 1 May 1998.

Currently most first mortgages used for the purchase of a house are exempt, although from 2002 the Financial Services Authority (see page 164) will regulate mortgages. Other exemptions include certain agreements where the number of payments is limited to a maximum of four within 12 months and some 'running account' credit agreements such as charge cards. There are also a number of so-called 'low-interest' exemptions. Finally, there are a number of miscellaneous minor exemptions, for example for consumers who have agreements for meters owned by electricity suppliers.

Usually credit agreements state clearly if they are regulated by the CCA, but if you are not sure, seek advice from one of the agencies listed in Chapter 1.

If an agreement *is* regulated, the creditor must give you a copy of the agreement if you ask for one. If the creditor doesn't, this may make the agreement unenforceable. This often arises in the context of catalogue agreements (see page 15).

A regulated agreement must include the following details:

- name and address of debtor and creditor
- all charges
- penalties for default
- cash price of goods or services
- goods supplied
- amount of any deposit
- amount of credit
- charge for credit
- rate of interest
- repayment details (amount, frequency)
- debtor's rights to cancel or terminate

In order to ascertain your rights in relation to a credit agreement, you need to establish whether or not it is regulated. This in turn will help to establish:

- your and the creditor's rights to terminate the agreement;
- what procedures the creditor must follow to be able to sue you for money or return of goods; and
- whether you have the right to apply to the Court for time to pay (see *Time Orders* on page 111).

There is an important difference between 'fixed' and 'running' account credit. In a 'fixed' sum agreement the amount borrowed is as set out in the original credit agreement. 'Running' account credit allows a debtor to receive goods or services, from time to time, up to an agreed credit limit. An example is a shop credit card, and a debtor can continually borrow up to the credit limit.

Parties to an agreement

There is a distinction between 'debtor–creditor–supplier' agreements and more straightforward 'debtor–creditor' agreements. In the first, the creditor is financing the transaction but is not supplying goods or services (eg Hire Purchase). On the other hand, the debtor–creditor agreement may be a simple loan of money.

Charges for credit

The 1974 *Consumer Credit Act* introduced the *annual percentage rate* (APR) as a concept so that people could compare the cost of different sources of credit. The interest rate, for example, may represent only part of the cost of credit. There could also be:

- administrative charges;
- documentation fees; and
- maintenance charges.

The APR should include all of these. It must be included in advertisements for credit.

Cancelling or terminating credit agreements

Individuals who have taken on credit commitments and changed their minds, for example because they have decided that they cannot afford the repayments, have a limited amount of time (usually 5 to 7 days) to cancel these agreements. In some cases it is not possible to cancel an agreement at all.

In practice, most people who are looking for advice about debt problems are already past these time limits. However, they may still be able to terminate the agreement. This is a particularly important issue when dealing with HP agreements, where termination by the debtor can be more advantageous than termination by the lender. If you are having problems with paying an HP agreement, seek advice from one of the agencies listed in Chapter 1, as the issues are complex.

Default – what happens?

Where the credit agreement is a regulated one, and the consumer does not keep to the agreed repayments, the creditor must serve a Default Notice before they can start Court proceedings.

The Default Notice terminates the agreement unless the default is corrected. It is usually a demand for immediate repayment of the whole debt and all other money due (interest, charges etc) although it may only call in the arrears. In the case of Hire Purchase or conditional sale agreements, it is also a demand for the return of the goods supplied.

A Default Notice has to be in a particular form laid down by the *Consumer Credit Act* 1974 (CCA). It must tell you how you can make good the breach of the agreement, usually by making an outstanding payment. In particular, it must state how much to pay to whom and by when.

If you comply with this notice, the creditor cannot take any further action. If, however, you cannot, because you have no money, you may be able to apply for a *Time Order* (see page 111).

A Default Notice is not necessary in certain circumstances, including:

- where the agreement is not regulated;
- where a creditor is restricting or preventing you from using further credit, for example by demanding the return of a credit card;
- where goods bought on HP, conditional sale, or on hire, have been disposed of without the authority of the creditor; and
- where the agreement is void because of misrepresentation or fraud.

Where the creditor fails to comply with any of the requirements of the CCA, you have several possible remedies, including for example seeking an order to prevent the creditor from removing goods, or seeking damages for wrongful repossession of the goods. If you think that this may apply to you, seek advice from a specialist money adviser, a legal aid solicitor, law centre or trading standards office.

*K*ey points

- Debts can be divided into **non-priority** (eg bank loans, credit cards) and **high priority** (eg utilities, mortgage, rent).

- There is a wide variety of sources of credit and loans from which debts can arise.

- If you have a consumer debt, you may have rights under the Consumer Credit Act.

- Always compare the APRs before taking out a loan. Don't assume that 0 per cent interest is the best, as the goods may be more expensive than elsewhere.

- If you are thinking of changing your mortgage, always consult an independent financial adviser.

- Always make sure that you understand the terms and conditions before taking out a loan – insist on an explanation if you are not clear.

3 The elements of debt management

This chapter covers the elements involved in managing debt, namely:

- *information gathering;*
- *crisis management;*
- *income maximisation;*
- *checking liability; and*
- *analysing expenditure.*

Information gathering

It is essential to be clear about the extent of the problem. Unfortunately many people do not feel confident enough to disclose the full amount of their debts when they first contact an advice agency. You should try to give your money adviser a full picture of your finances otherwise they will not be able to give you the best advice. The best way to do this is to bring all your correspondence and other information about your debts to the advice agency.

Identifying creditors

It is pointless to try to deal with creditors one at a time, as it is necessary to ensure that all creditors are dealt with fairly according to an accepted pro rata model – ie that everyone will receive a proportion of what you can afford to pay, based on a formula which is fair to everyone.

Establishing amounts owed

Add up all your debts, including interest. Don't forget to include debts with which you are up to date. The total may come as a shock to you but try not to lose confidence at this stage; your adviser can explain what will happen next. It is important to have a full picture of the situation in order to begin to work out how to tackle the debts.

Calculating income

The calculation should include all your household income from all sources (such as State benefits, pensions, interest from any savings etc).

Crisis management

Whether or not any particular debt requires emergency action depends in part upon the stage in formal debt recovery proceedings that a creditor has reached. For example, if the creditor has been to Court, and an order has been made which permits the creditor to use the *bailiffs* to remove your belongings (see Chapter 6), this will necessitate prompt action to negotiate payment by instalments.

Income maximisation

Maximising your income to its fullest potential is a priority.

State benefits

Potential sources for increasing income if you are approaching retirement or are already in retirement include:

- State Retirement Pension
- Housing Benefit
- Council Tax Benefit
- Income Support (also called Minimum Income Guarantee)

The State Retirement Pension is paid to people who have reached pension age (currently 60 for women, 65 for men) and is based on your National Insurance contributions record. If a reduced pension is offered by the Benefits Agency, ask the National Insurance Contributions Agency (NICO) about your contribution record (see address on page 165).

Whether you are entitled to a State Pension or not, you may be able to claim benefits depending on your income and savings. There are detailed eligibility conditions and rules on the treatment of income and capital for Income Support (Minimum Income Guarantee) for example but you should make sure that you are not losing out.

There are also social security benefits available to people with disabilities and those who look after them:

■ Disability Living Allowance (DLA) is a disability benefit which is not means tested and which has a care component and a mobility component. It is for people who become ill or disabled and make a claim before the age of 65.

■ Attendance Allowance is for people over the age of 65 and is also not means tested. It has day and/or night conditions which affect the rate at which the benefit is paid.

■ Invalid Care Allowance (ICA) is a benefit for people who are unable to work full-time because they are caring for a severely disabled person for at least 35 hours a week. Currently, you must have started caring and have become entitled to ICA before the age of 65, although once you receive ICA it can continue to be paid after the age of 65. In the future it is planned to change the law to enable carers aged 65 and over to claim.

Detailed information about entitlement to State benefits is available in the Age Concern annual publication *Your Rights* (see page 168). A local advice agency will be able to carry out a thorough benefits check for you.

Other sources of income

Other possible sources of income which you may wish to consider include:

■ Renting a room to students or others who may be looking to live in a homely atmosphere. You will need to consider what effect this may have if you receive benefits. You should also think about whether you wish to share your home with a stranger.

■ Looking at how you pay your bills and whether you are being charged too much. It may be there are cheaper ways of paying.

■ Checking to see if you have any policies which are maturing or any possible windfalls from building societies etc which are now public limited companies.

- Checking your tax coding; ie making certain that you are receiving the correct allowances, and looking at whether or not you should be paying Income Tax.
- Taking on part-time work if you are able. However, always check first to make sure that it wouldn't affect any benefits you receive.
- Checking whether any savings which you had put away for a rainy day, could/should be used to clear off any debts. Discuss this with an independent financial adviser first before deciding.
- If you own your home, considering whether you want to release some of the equity. If you are aged 60 or over, you may be able to use the capital value of your home to raise cash – while continuing to live in it – by taking out a home reversion scheme, a home income plan, a roll-up loan plan or one of the new type of equity release plans. In general, the older you are, the higher the income or capital you will receive from these schemes, and there are only a few schemes open to people under the age of 65. You will need legal and financial advice before entering into a scheme. Age Concern publishes a book, *Using Your Home as Capital* (see page 168), and a Factsheet *Raising Income or Capital from Your Home* (see page 169 for details of how to obtain Age Concern factsheets) which give more details on equity release schemes.
- Contacting your former employer's welfare section to see if they can make payments from benevolent funds.
- Contacting your union to see if it has a hardship fund.
- Approaching other charities or benevolent funds to see if they can offer any assistance. They often help people in particular circumstances, such as people with particular health problems or disabilities or people who live in a particular parish. To find out more information you could contact a local advice agency or look in your library at the *Charities Digest* or *A Guide to Grants for Individuals in Need*. The Association of Charity Officers (incorporating the Occupational Benevolent Funds Alliance) and Charity Search are two national organisations that can help put people in contact with charities and benevolent funds – their addresses are on pages 162 and 163.
- Checking if your spouse is entitled to benefits.

Checking liability

Before payment is made in respect of a debt, it is important to make sure that you are legally liable for it. This is always worth checking. For example, some creditors may (wrongly) try to recover a debt from the widow or widower of the borrower. There is a crucial difference between a creditor legitimately making a claim against the estate of the deceased, on the one hand, and attempting to persuade their spouse to accept liability where the debt was not in joint names. If a borrower dies with no assets, leaving debts, there is *no* obligation on the part of their spouse to accept any liability.

Analysing expenditure

You need to work out your expenditure as well as your income. An example of how to go about this is set out below. Drawing up a *Personal Budget* will help you see how you can (or cannot) match your income to your expenditure. You can also use it to help explain your situation to your creditors.

Make certain that you have maximised your income (see pages 24–26). The money adviser will help you with this. If you have been granted a new benefit, such as Attendance Allowance, it may take some time before payment is made to you. You can always recalculate your income later. In the meantime, tell creditors your current income and that you will review the overall situation at a later date.

Essential expenditure

The objective is to realistically examine your basic everyday expenditure, ignoring any arrears for the moment. Many people tend to underestimate their basic living expenses; make certain that you have allowed for the actual costs.

There are certain items that are clearly essential. These include:

- **Housekeeping** – eg food, toiletries, cleaning materials, medicines.
- **Fuel costs** – a realistic estimate of fuel costs is essential. If possible, try to get your last four bills, average them out and convert to fit the period of your Personal Budget (usually a year).

- **Rent** – this means current rent payable after calculation of Housing Benefit. Do not include contributions towards rent arrears as these are a priority debt and will be dealt with later.
- **Council Tax** – ie ongoing liability; not arrears, which should be treated as priority debts.
- **Mortgage** – normal monthly payment, plus endowment premiums for example.
- **Secured loans** – current repayments on any loan secured against your house.
- **Insurance** – life and household contents insurance (and buildings, if not included under mortgage).
- **Telephone** – the most important means of communication for many people, particularly where it is required for health reasons. Try and get your last four bills, as with fuel above.
- **TV rental/TV licence** – some creditors may take the view that the television is not an essential. (If you are over 75, your licence will be free.)
- **Travel** – travel to and from shops, visiting relatives and friends on a reasonable basis, etc. Cars may be accepted as essential for mobility in a rural area and/or for reasons of health or disability. Expenditure includes a mixture of fuel, road tax, insurance, MOT, etc.
- **Clothing** – a figure of £200 per annum for adults may be reasonable. If you have special needs because of disability or size, then the figure may need to increase accordingly.
- **Newspapers and leisure, hobbies, gardening, pets, etc** – reasonable amounts can be included for these and included under the housekeeping heading.
- **Water** – although domestic premises can no longer be disconnected for non-payment of water debt, an allowance still needs to be made for ongoing water and sewerage charges.
- **Cigarettes and alcohol** – if you smoke and feel unable to stop, it is highly unlikely that you will feel able to stop in a stressful situation, such as being in multiple debt. It is unrealistic to expect anyone to completely give up smoking and/or drinking

overnight. However, you may wish to consider how your creditors will react, and perhaps try to reduce your intake.

■ **Sundries/emergencies**.

It is very important that you include all your expenditure and are realistic in what you say you will spend. Try to allow something for the unexpected, such as the washing machine breaking down for example.

To draw up a Personal Budget, you should do the following:

■ List all your income in the first section. Make sure that you use *either* monthly or weekly figures. If, for example, you receive benefit which is paid weekly and have a pension which is paid monthly, then you need to choose whether to use weekly or monthly figures. Do not mix the two.

■ To convert weekly figures to monthly figures you should multiply the weekly figure by 52 and divide by 12.

■ To convert monthly figures to weekly figures you should multiply the monthly figure by 12 and divide by 52.

■ You should then list all your expenditure, once again making sure that you do not mix weekly and monthly figures. It is very important that you are realistic about your expenditure in this section. Do not include payments that you are making to either your priority or non-priority creditors, as there is space to do this later in the form.

You may be able to identify obvious areas for cutting your expenditure. You may need to discuss this with a money adviser. The most important rule in identifying essential expenditure is to come up with a realistic figure that you feel able to stick to, especially for the long-term. Clearly, in order for you to 'balance the books', including making payments to your creditors, your income must be more than your expenditure – a money adviser will still be able to assist you even if it isn't.

Once you have found yourself on surer footing, it is helpful to stop and take stock and look at what you can do to avoid the worry of being in debt in the future. Some golden rules are:

1 If you think things are getting on top of you, go and see a money adviser.
2 Don't go on hoping that the problems will go away – they won't, so seek advice.
3 If you don't want to seek help from a money adviser, write to all your creditors right away and tell them you have a problem.
4 Try to obtain up-to-date regular statements from your bank. Ask them to send them to you weekly – provided, of course, that they don't charge you more for doing so.
5 Try to budget using your Personal Budget and allow a cushion (some money which you don't have earmarked for anything) which could be used in an emergency.
6 Look at paying your fuel bills on a more regular basis and even out the peaks and troughs. Ask a relative to read your meter to check that you are not consuming far more fuel than you are budgeting for.

*K*ey points

- Check whether you are claiming your full entitlement to State benefits.

- Check whether you can maximise your income in any other way.

- Check whether you are actually liable for a debt (ie whether it is in your name).

- Draw up an accurate income and expenditure sheet (Personal Budget) to negotiate with your creditors.

4 Prioritising debts and dealing with emergencies

This chapter covers:

- *The importance of prioritising debt*
- *Identifying priority debt*
- *Which debts are a priority and why*
- *Guidance on prioritising your debts*
- *Dealing with emergencies*

The importance of prioritising debt

When faced with financial difficulties, most people feel swamped by the situation and experience feelings of confusion over how to regain control. It is important to prioritise debts so as not to pay the 'wrong' ones and then find yourself out of a home for example. This chapter discusses reorganising payment of debts in an organised and practical manner and preventing crisis situations from developing in the future.

Creditors pursue debts in various ways and it may not always be clear to you what action they are intending to take or, indeed, what stage of the recovery process they are at. If you have missed payments to a creditor you may have been sent letters or received telephone calls which can be distressing.

Telephone calls and letters are often standard procedure by creditors who want to bring the matter to your attention. Don't be tempted into making 'knee-jerk' offers, or agreeing to payments that you can't manage, simply to get the person off the phone. But don't ignore the situation as this will only cause more worry in the long term and can allow the situation to get worse. Remember that there is always a solution to the problem. If you need help, contact one of the agencies listed in Chapter 1.

When faced with more than one creditor demanding payments, you need to look at the bigger picture and the long-term solution. Prioritising debt is essential in the organisation of your finances and will help you to regain control.

Identifying priority debt

A debt is not necessarily a priority simply because a demand letter has been received. It will all depend upon the nature of the debt, the recovery methods available to the creditor, and your individual circumstances. When assessing a debt's priority, you therefore need to examine:

- The severity of action available to the creditor – ie what action they can legally take to recover the debt from you. This might be Court action, imprisonment, eviction, your bank account being 'attached' (ie frozen) or the seizing of goods by a bailiff. There is little point in making payments to your bank overdraft your highest priority if you neglect your rent and risk eviction just because a letter from your landlord appears easier to ignore than the threats of your bank to take you to court.
- Your individual circumstances and needs. For example if you live in a rural area you may be more dependent on your car than someone with adequate access to public transport.
- The recovery policies of particular creditors.

As explained in the previous chapter, examine all your outgoings and decide which are your essentials. If necessary, seek free professional help with budgeting (see Chapter 1).

Which debts are a priority and why

Protecting your home – top priority

Rent arrears

Rent arrears are a priority because they can lead to your being forced to leave your home (eviction). Depending on the type of tenancy, your landlord can take legal steps to evict you if you have failed to pay your rent.

Rent arrears may have built up for a number of reasons. If you have a low income, you should check whether or not you are entitled to *Housing Benefit* or if the amount you have been awarded is correct. Advice agencies and law centres will be able to help you with this. In some cases you may be able to claim backdating of the benefit and thereby reduce your arrears. Advice agencies can also advise you on your housing rights and help you to negotiate with your landlord.

If your rent arrears are the result of a Housing Benefit overpayment being reclaimed, then your landlord might not be able to raise eviction proceedings – seek expert advice as soon as possible. It will be easier, and usually cheaper, to deal with rent arrears prior to Court action.

If you are having long-term difficulties paying your rent, check your outgoings and, in particular, payments that you are making to non-priority creditors. These should be reduced in order for you to pay your rent first. Other long-term solutions may have to include moving to a house or flat that is more manageable in terms of size and cost.

Mr and Mrs McDougall have lived in their four-bedroomed home for 20 years, but their children have all left home. They have rent charges of £300 per month and Council Tax of £120 per month. In addition, their heating costs are very high as the house is old, large and badly insulated. A move to a new one-bedroomed home reduces their rent to £160 per month and their Council Tax to £60 per month, with heating costs lowered by around £25 per month. This saves them around £2,700 a year.

If you receive Income Support (also known as Minimum Income Guarantee), you may be entitled to financial assistance with removal costs. If you are disabled, you may be eligible for a grant from the *Social Fund* for items to help you remain living independently in the community. If you have high heating costs or your house lacks adequate heating, seek information on heating insulation and advice on how to reduce fuel costs and on any heating grants that may be available. The Age Concern Factsheet *Help with Heating* is available free from the address on page 169.

Mortgage arrears and secured loans

Non-payment of your mortgage and any other loans secured on it (second mortgages or further advances) are a priority because they can lead via the Courts to the lender repossessing and evicting you from your home. The lender can then sell the house to pay off the outstanding debt. If the proceeds of the sale do not pay off all of the debt, you will still be liable for the remainder.

Secured loans and second mortgages are similar to first mortgages in that they give the lender the right to force the sale of your home to pay off the debt if you cannot make your payments.

Some lenders may initially consider your mortgage arrears in isolation without taking into account your other problems affecting your ability to pay. It is imperative that they look at your other outgoings and essential expenditure. The Mortgage Code states that lenders must look at an individual's overall situation when they are in arrears – any solution to your debt problem must be sustainable and take into account the full picture.

If you have mortgage arrears you have the following options:

- resolve the payment problems and remain in the house;
- apply to the lender for access to a mortgage rescue scheme (see page 37);
- minimise the shortfall in payments and sell the home voluntarily;
- give the lender voluntary possession (by handing in the keys); or
- allow the matter to be settled by the Court.

It may be possible to agree a change in the terms of your mortgage. Generally a lender expects you to come up with the proposals to clear/reduce the debt rather than making suggestions itself. Offer only what you can reasonably afford; concentrate on the arrears and ask for flexibility to make the mortgage more manageable.

It is essential that you continue to make regular payments to demonstrate goodwill. Your proposals must be realistic and designed to repay the mortgage within a reasonable period of time which could be within the remaining period of the mortgage. You need to make any proposals in writing and any agreements should be confirmed in writing by the lender.

The lender's decision on whether to accept your proposals will be determined by the extent to which the arrears can be controlled.

When writing to your lender, you should be as open and frank as possible about the reasons for your financial problems. Include the following details:

- the reasons for your difficulties (eg redundancy);
- whether the problem is likely to be long or short term; and
- show how at least the interest will be paid to control the arrears.

Be reassured that in general most mortgage arrears can be dealt with either through negotiation with the lender or at the possession hearing.

Reducing the arrears

You may have to find ways of reducing the arrears by making either a lump-sum payment or a series of regular payments in addition to your normal mortgage payments, for example over 12 months but it can be much longer – the Court can allow any length of time provided that the arrears are cleared before the end of the mortgage term.

If you have endowment policies not linked to your mortgage, you may be able to get a good price for 'assigning' them (commonly known as 'selling' them) to a broker. The policy continues to run but the purchaser pays the premiums instead of you. The purchaser receives the proceeds of the policy when eventually it matures. Simply cashing in an endowment policy early is not usually a good idea as you are likely to lose a substantial amount of the potential value of the policy. If you are considering either of these options, you should get advice from an independent financial adviser, although you may have to pay a fee for this.

It is usually unwise to take out an extra loan to repay mortgage arrears. Many such refinancing or re-mortgaging deals have a fixed high interest rate and penalties for early redemption (eg three months additional interest).

Another option is to ask the lender to add the arrears to the mortgage (known as 'capitalising the arrears'). Your lender may consider this if your arrears are still manageable and there is sufficient *equity* value in your house.

Whatever else you do, it is important that you try to pay at least the interest on the loan to avoid the *total* debt increasing to a completely unmanageable level, where the lender is likely to move to repossession. Your lender may be willing to accept less than the full interest payments if you are trying to sell the property. Even a nominal payment may be acceptable if the property is being actively marketed.

If possible, you may wish to consider switching to a repayment mortgage, which may be cheaper than the costs of an endowment. Alternately, you could look for an interest-only mortgage. It will usually be necessary to arrange life insurance, which can be difficult for older people. You will still need to make arrangements to pay the capital sum borrowed at the end of the term either with a new endowment policy or other scheme (such as a pension or an ISA) or, ultimately, if none of these is possible, by sale of the house.

If you already have a repayment mortgage, options to explore include:

- reducing payments by extending the repayment term; or
- reducing monthly payments by paying a lump sum, payment holidays or switching to interest-only payments.

Check whether you have a payment protection plan. This is a form of insurance designed to meet all or part of your mortgage costs if you lose your job or are too ill to work. Payment protection policies usually do not pay out for at least the first 60 days of unemployment or illness.

Check also whether you are eligible to receive *Income Support* as you may then also get help with your mortgage interest payments. The rules are complex, but are more favourable for older people – one rate applies for people aged 60–74 and a higher rate for those aged 75–79 – and you should get advice from one of the sources listed in Chapter 1.

Mortgage rescue schemes

If your arrears are not too high you may have the option of arranging for a finance company, housing association or local authority to enter into a mortgage rescue scheme. Unfortunately these schemes are still very rare. They enable you to remain in your own home as a tenant (either wholly or partly). The housing association or local authority purchases your mortgage and pays off the arrears to the original lender. You then become a tenant or co-owner of the property, with the option to buy back your home in the future should your circumstances improve.

To be eligible you must normally fulfil the following criteria:

- arrears must not be unduly high (offering protection to the lender in the event of a sale);
- you must have a particular reason for wanting to continue to live in the house (eg you have relatives living nearby); and
- rehousing by the local authority would be difficult.

Seek expert advice from a solicitor, law centre or Shelter (see address on page 166) if you are thinking of entering into such a scheme as there can be disadvantages (such as legal costs) and you may need assistance in persuading an authority or housing association to enter into the scheme with you.

Selling the house

If your house is sold after repossession by the lender, it is likely to sell for no more than 85 per cent of the price that you might have obtained if you had sold it yourself. If your lender sells the property, they decide how it is to be marketed and what offer should be accepted although they have a general duty to try to obtain the 'best' price. It is better to try for a voluntary sale of the property if possession proceedings and an enforced sale are otherwise inevitable. Your lender's written authority is required for a sale if you will not be able to repay the loan in full.

If when you bought your house your deposit was less than 25 per cent of the purchase price and you took out your mortgage recently, you may have had to pay for mortgage indemnity insurance. This insurance is arranged between your lender and an insurance company at the start of the mortgage. It is to indemnify the lender (not you) against losses up to a certain limit, if the property is sold at a loss. If the insurance company has paid out on a mortgage indemnity claim, it is entitled to claim the money back from you.

Protecting yourself and your belongings

Fines, Compensation Orders, Council Tax arrears and maintenance payments

Non-payment of Magistrates Court fines, *Compensation Orders*, Council Tax or Community Charge arrears or maintenance payments carries the threat of imprisonment as well as possible loss of personal possessions which may be seized by *bailiffs* and various other methods of enforcement such as attachment of earnings and deductions from Income Support.

Imprisonment may be used if the magistrates decide that there has been 'wilful refusal or culpable neglect'. These are legal terms and refer to the refusal to pay when there are the means available or where a debtor has chosen to use money for other purposes which are not reasonable (eg for non-essential items). Expert advice from one of the agencies listed in Chapter 1 should always be sought if Magistrates Court action is being taken against you.

VAT arrears, Income Tax and NI contributions

If you owe VAT arrears, Income Tax or National Insurance (NI) contributions, they should also be treated as a priority. Seek expert advice immediately. The creditor should be contacted as soon as possible and an offer of repayment made. The Inland Revenue and Customs and Excise have the power to seize your goods to pay for the debt without the need to obtain a Court order first.

The Inland Revenue can use the *Magistrates Court* or the *County Court* and obtain an order against you for payment of any debt. If you do not keep to the terms of any order, you may be imprisoned if the Court decides that you were financially able to keep to its terms, but chose not to. This is on the grounds that you are in contempt of Court. (VAT debt can only lead to imprisonment if there has been fraudulent evasion.) Personal *bankruptcy* proceedings can also be instigated for failure to pay either of these debts.

Protecting your health and well-being

Gas and electricity

Non-payment can lead to disconnection and therefore the loss of your supply. These debts are therefore usually treated as a priority. (See page 45 for more information on disconnection.)

Debts owed to friends and family

These may be a personal priority if they threaten established relationships with your friends and family or other sources of emotional support, leading to the possibility of isolation. The priority given will depend entirely upon your individual circumstances.

Goods on Hire Purchase

Whether or not goods on *Hire Purchase* (see page 14) are treated as a priority debt depends on your individual circumstances and on the nature of the goods supplied. In deciding its priority, look at what the effects of losing the item would be and also if there are any alternatives. Are the goods an essential item or a luxury item? If they have been in your possession for some time, the creditor may decide that repossession of the item would not be worthwhile and they will therefore be more open to an agreement for a reduced payment. (See Chapter 5 for information on negotiating with your creditors.)

Guidance on prioritising your debts

To prioritise your debts, make a list of all your creditors and note what sanctions/legal action can be taken against you for recovery of the sum owed. Also note at what stage of recovery each debt is. Your debts should not be looked at in isolation from one another, as payments to one will affect your ability to pay another. There is little point in dealing with one emergency if this is going to create another one.

Mr Benedict has rent arrears and agrees to high repayments with his landlord in order to repay the arrears within six months. However, the repayments are so high that he finds that he is unable to pay his Council Tax. This leads to the Council instructing bailiffs to seize his goods.

Mr Benedict should have looked at all his debts and negotiated with his landlord to repay the rent arrears over a longer period at a lower level. This would have enabled him to keep up to date with his Council Tax and avoid recovery action for these payments. He should also have told his local authority about his problems with paying his Council Tax.

If your rent arrears are low, and your landlord is reasonable and/or unlikely or unable to take Court action, this situation may make the Council Tax arrears a higher priority. It all depends on individual circumstances. If you are unsure, always seek further advice and assistance from one of the agencies listed in Chapter 1, especially when you have multiple creditors to deal with. Always bear in mind the importance of priority debts given the sanctions that can be imposed but you need to negotiate the amount you can repay. Also, just because a debt is a priority this does not mean that you must pay the sum being demanded by the creditor, as it may not be practical or reasonable to do so.

Personal prioritising

You may have given some debts personal priority despite the fact that the legal sanctions for their non-payment are less powerful than for other debts. For example, bank loans are frequently prioritised over other debts and essential payments. This usually occurs when you take out a loan with your bank and it arranges for the repayments to be made from your current account. This loan operates in a similar way to a direct debit coming off each month except that it cannot be cancelled when you choose. This method of repayment becomes a problem at times of financial difficulties, as most banks will continue to make the deduction from your current account even if you do not have the money in your account to meet the payments and so you incur extra charges of interest. These repayments can be hard to renegotiate as the bank has control of your finances. Often the only way to stop payments if the bank refuses to reduce them is to stop using the account and open another account elsewhere. Eventually the bank should see sense and stop making the payments to the loan.

Many people feel a loyalty to their banks, especially if they have been with them for a number of years. However, you should weigh up your feelings of loyalty against how helpful your bank is being during your period of financial difficulty. Remember that simply allowing you to increase your overdraft is not necessarily in your best long-term interests and so may not be as helpful as it might appear. There are now many more banks and building societies in the marketplace looking for your business, so changing your account is one way for you to regain control of your finances and deal with priority debts. However, it is not always easy to open an account when you are in debt, especially if you don't have much money.

Another example of debts being given a high priority which may not be practical in the long term, are those that are collected by local agents calling at a person's home. Again there are often feelings of loyalty and also embarrassment or pressure due to the nature of the face to face relationship. Many agents work on commission and are therefore unwilling to reduce payments as this will lower their own income.

Remember that you are only one of many customers that the collector or agent has and that the parent company should recognise that from time to time their customers will have financial difficulties. Usually the money owed is for personal loans which have lesser sanctions available to the creditor than for other debts. If negotiations with the agent have not succeeded in reducing the payments, contact either the local branch or the head office of the organisation. (See Chapter 5 for further advice on negotiating with your creditors.)

Often debts are given priority over others because the end appears in sight and there is a feeling that this will mean one less debt that you don't have to worry about. An example of this would be where there are only six months remaining on a five year loan. Tempting as it may seem to carry on the payments to this debt, it may cause greater stress in the long term if you are unable to pay other creditors who have more serious sanctions available to them.

Prioritising this kind of debt is only possible if you have a limited number of creditors and if they are willing to suspend action for a few months whilst you pay this other creditor. In practice they will rarely do this. The long-term solution is to pay the first creditor lower repayments in order to also pay your other creditors an acceptable amount. Although the debt will take longer to repay, you will be more likely to save yourself the stress of being pursued by the other creditors.

Mr and Mrs Taylor had always managed their money successfully; although things were tight, they always paid their bills on time. Unfortunately, they had only managed because of Mr Taylor's over-time. When this stopped, they tried to carry on with the payments that they had always made – they would use their cash income to pay things like the mortgage and then use their credit cards and overdraft to cover their weekly household bills. A couple of times Mr Taylor didn't send the mortgage payments to the building soci-ety, hoping that he would be able to catch up later; he didn't want to worry his wife and so didn't tell her. Things came to a head when Mrs Taylor opened a letter from the bank explaining that the direct debits for their Council Tax and gas had not been paid as they had gone over their agreed overdraft limit by £500.

The couple sat down and looked at all their commitments. Mr Taylor told his wife that the mortgage had not been paid for two months and why. Mrs Taylor had seen a television programme about debt and contacted one of the telephone numbers that had been given out at the end of the programme. Using the information that they were sent, the Taylors realised that they had been trying to keep up with both their priority and non-priori-ty payments when their income had gone down. They drew up an initial Personal Budget, putting down all their essential expendi-ture. This showed them what was left to use to pay all their debts. They then contacted their mortgage lender and agreed to pay an extra £20 a month to clear the arrears that had appeared because of the missed payments. They opened a new bank account and got Mr Taylor's wages paid into that account. They then set up new direct debits to pay all their essentials. The council agreed to accept an extra payment of £5 a month to catch up with the month that they had missed. The gas company agreed to alter the direct debit by £2.

Once Mr and Mrs Taylor had dealt with all the important bills, they turned their attention to their credit debts. Including their bank overdraft, they owed £10,000 to six creditors. Although they could not pay the creditors back at the original rate, they did have some money to offer to their creditors. They calculated pro rata offers (see page 68) using the information that they had been sent. They then wrote to all their creditors explaining that Mr Taylor had lost his overtime and asking them to agree to reduced payments and to freeze interest. The Taylors sent a copy of their Personal Budget with each letter so that the creditors could see what they genuinely could afford. Four creditors agreed to the offers straightaway. The other two passed the debt onto debt collection agencies. Mr Taylor sent further letters and the collection agencies agreed to accept the reduced payments. Although the Taylors knew that it would now take longer to repay their debts, they were happy that they felt in control of their finances again.

Prioritising your debts is a practical way of reorganising your finances and regaining control and peace of mind. However, the prioritisation can be affected by emergency situations, either before or during the process. In the next section we look at emergency situations and how to deal with these as they arise.

Dealing with emergencies

What amounts to an emergency depends upon a number of factors, including:

- the nature of the creditor;
- the threat or sanction that is available to them;
- individual perceptions of what amounts to an emergency; and
- subjective influences such as your own personal fears and emotional states.

Knowledge of the recovery process that is used by creditors, as well as the remedies that are available to you, will allow you to take control of the situation and avoid a crisis.

If imminent, the following require immediate attention in order to avoid:

- loss of the supply of utilities
- loss of possessions
- loss of your home
- loss of your liberty

Fuel disconnection

Failure to pay the fuel companies may eventually result in disconnection of your supply. However, households where all the occupants are of pensionable age (currently 60 for women and 65 for men) should not be disconnected between October and March unless it is clear that you have sufficient money to pay. If you receive a disconnection notice, contact the supplier immediately, who will discuss methods of repayment. Before accepting that you owe the sums claimed and agreeing to a repayment programme, check the following factors:

- Are you liable?
- Is the bill accurate?
- Would a pre-payment meter help?
- What other ways of paying are there?

Remember that even in cases of disconnection it is never too late to try and contact the supplier and arrange repayments. Even if the supplier is at your door to disconnect your supply, you should be able to stop the disconnection by paying the sum owed if this is available to you, or you can ask to be allowed to phone the relevant department whilst they wait. If the disconnection has already been carried out, contact the company involved, which should reconnect your supply once a repayment arrangement has been made. Unfortunately, there may be a charge for this.

Liability

Check whether or not you are legally liable to pay the arrears. In most cases this will be fairly straightforward. If the bill is in your name and you have been supplied with gas or electricity, then you will probably be liable. If the bill has no name or is addressed to the occupier, it will depend on your circumstances and who else occupies your home. Liability is then determined by factors such as:

- your status in the home (eg whether you are the head of the household);
- control of income; and
- your actual use of fuel.

You might not be legally liable if the bill is in the name of someone who originally gave notice to the supplier that they required a supply, provided that you have not accepted liability yourself.

Even when a bill is in a spouse's name, it has been successfully argued in an electricity supply case that the other spouse is not liable. In one case a wife of a deceased man was found not to be liable for arrears accumulated prior to his death. This may also be the case when a spouse or partner has left the shared home. If you are unsure of your liability for any arrears, seek advice from a Citizens Advice Bureau (CAB), money advice centre or law centre.

Accuracy of the bill

Check your bill details and make sure that the readings are correct. If you have recently moved, the bill may well be estimated based on consumption by the previous occupiers. If your bill has been overestimated, most suppliers should agree to revise the bill based on the exact reading that you provide. They may want to come and make their own reading for confirmation.

If there are disputes concerning the bill, you should not be disconnected prior to the matter being resolved. If you are satisfied that you *are* liable for the arrears, you should discuss your repayment options with your supplier.

Always think about your other financial commitments before agreeing to the level of any repayments. Using your *Personal Budget* (see pages 27–29) will help you to negotiate a level that you can afford and avoid emergencies in the future.

Pre-payment meters

Many suppliers offer pre-payment meters to customers who have arrears. This avoids future arrears occurring as you pay before you use the fuel (usually by buying cards from shops or post offices etc). The main disadvantage is that it can result in 'self-disconnection' if you are unable to buy cards at any point due to lack of money or because you become housebound through illness or severe weather conditions; the supply is automatically cut when your current credit runs out. Most meters have an emergency supply but these are limited.

If a meter is installed as a result of arrears, it will be adjusted so that the arrears are collected on the basis of a fixed sum each week regardless of how much fuel you use.

When agreeing to a repayment plan for your arrears do not be 'bullied' into accepting a pre-payment meter if you don't want one.

Other ways of paying arrears

Other options include spreading the cost of the arrears over a set period. Suppliers should consider your ability to pay above the length of time it will take to recover the arrears. If you are in receipt of Income Support (Minimum Income Guarantee), you have the option of asking the Benefits Agency to make direct deductions at a fixed rate from your Income Support each week to the supplier. If you are on a low income or other benefits, you should ask to be allowed to repay the sum at a similar level to the Income Support fixed rate.

Avoiding future emergencies

Spread the cost of fuel consumption over the whole year so that you are not faced with high winter bills. Most companies will offer fixed payment budget schemes, whereby they estimate your yearly consumption and spread the cost over the whole year, so that you pay the same amount in the summer months as you do in the winter.

Ask for advice on reducing your bill through energy efficiency measures. Many companies offer telephone advice or will send someone to your home to discuss how you could reduce your bill.

Your local authority or advice centre will have information on heating grants and other schemes in your area. Many of these schemes offer assistance with installation of heating systems and draughtproofing. If you are on benefits, the costs may be covered in whole or part by the body offering the scheme. There are no regular weekly social security payments towards fuel bills but there are Winter Fuel Payments for pensioner households and Cold Weather Payments. For further information, see Age Concern Factsheet 1 *Help with Heating*, which is available from the address on page 169.

Severe hardship

In some cases of severe hardship, you may be successful in requesting that a company *write off* the arrears. This will depend entirely upon individual circumstances and the policy of the supplier.

Regulatory bodies

If your fuel supplier is acting unreasonably, you could also contact the regulatory body (OFGEM) at the address on page 166. OFGEM can deal with various issues and disputes between you and the supplier. It will usually expect that you have made an attempt to resolve any dispute through direct negotiations with the supplier. If these have failed, OFGEM has wide powers to enforce your legal rights. You do not have to pay for its assistance.

As well as rights in law, you may also have additional rights as a customer via individual company policies. Telephone or write to the company involved in the dispute for copies of its policy and information on your consumer rights.

Water disconnection

Domestic water supply can no longer be disconnected. As with the fuel companies, contact the supplier in order to come to a repayment arrangement. Income Support claimants can request direct deductions. If the water company is being unreasonable, contact the regulatory body, which is the Office of Water Services (OFWAT), at the address on page 166. Many water companies now have customer welfare units or separate charitable trusts to whom application can be made for a grant to clear water and sewerage debts. Check with your water company.

Bailiffs and the seizure of goods

Bailiffs are used for the collection of unpaid debts where the creditor is seeking to seize goods owned by the debtor in order to sell them for payment of the outstanding sum due. (See page 93 for further details on bailiffs and debt enforcement.)

Check the policy of the creditor regarding your individual circumstances. Local authorities collecting Council Tax have different policies, but many do not carry out seizure of goods if the debtor is on certain benefits or in cases of severe hardship.

For debts where there is a *County Court Judgment*, apply to the courts for time to pay and to suspend the warrant. This should be done as soon as possible after you have received notice that a warrant for the seizure of goods has been issued. (See Chapter 6 for further information.)

For debts where there is *High Court Judgment*, apply to the High Court for a stay of execution. A Hearing will be arranged to consider any repayment proposals. (Chapter 6 has further information on Court procedures and completing forms.)

In all other cases, including Council Tax arrears (where no application to Court is possible), contact the creditor direct to arrange repayments – this can be done at any stage of the process. It is advisable to make contact as soon as possible in order to avoid further action being taken against you. (In general creditors are more likely to take action when no contact is made.) Creditors may request a financial statement and will usually want to know the reasons for non-payment. You may be insured if non-payment is the result of certain illnesses or accident. Most insurance policies pay out for a set period (usually only six to twelve months). If the creditor is acting unreasonably or refuses to accept your offer, seek expert advice or assistance. (See also Chapter 5 for negotiating with your creditors.)

Imprisonment

Refusal to pay fines, Council Tax, Community Charge or maintenance can result in imprisonment. You will always be given a chance to explain your default at a hearing, and for the Court to assess your means.

The Magistrates Court will issue a warrant for your arrest either with or without bail. If with bail, you are required to 'surrender' yourself to your local police station and you will be given a date for a Court Hearing and allowed to return home. When attending Court you will not normally be held in the cells until your Hearing. You will be asked to attend a means enquiry hearing and given a form to complete either when the Hearing date is set or before the Hearing. You will need to take full details of your essential expenditure and a list of creditors and be prepared to justify any large amounts (such as the high cost of fuel to heat your home).

If the warrant is without bail, the police have the power of arrest and you will be held until your Court Hearing, which will usually be as soon as possible and should be within 24 hours or so. You will not normally receive a warrant without bail unless you have previously ignored warrants with bail. Seek expert advice and representation for your Hearing from a solicitor. A lay representative is not allowed to accompany you into the Magistrates Court.

Repossession and eviction

Landlords and lenders are legally obliged to inform you by letter of their intention to start possession action. Mortgage lenders will have set policies and standard letters warning of impending action. If your loan is regulated under the Consumer Credit Act, a *Default Notice* must also be served under the terms of the agreement.

If Court action is being taken, you will receive a summons which will state the time and date of the Hearing and the grounds/details of the action. This will include details of missed payments and other information concerning the agreement. The summons will also contain a form for you to reply to the summons, including whether or not you agree to the arrears figure and if you wish to make an offer of repayment. If you have negotiated any agreement with your lender/landlord, you should provide details of this agreement. Always ask your lender/landlord to provide written confirmation of any agreements made.

You are strongly advised to seek expert advice and/or representation with Court forms and any Hearing.

If a Possession Order and a *Warrant for Possession* has already been granted, you should make an immediate application for suspension of the warrant, unless there is time to make an agreement with the lender or landlord not to repossess the property. Many landlords will request a lump-sum payment as well as regular repayments before they will agree to this, but don't be afraid to try and negotiate lesser terms if you are unable to offer it.

Only obtain a loan from family, friends, or other sources as a last resort. You should consider these options carefully before deciding on them, and, if seeking loans from commercial sources, be aware of the interest rate that will be charged and any other charges. Obtaining a commercial loan often only makes the situation worse and you would be better off negotiating a smaller repayment.

Time Orders

In some circumstances you may be able to apply for a *Time Order* to prevent repossession for default on a secured loan regulated by the Consumer Credit Act 1974. Time Orders can alter interest and repayment rates on loans if these are deemed to be unfair or if there are extenuating circumstances that can be taken into account. You should seek assistance with any applications from an advice agency or law centre. If you are on a low income or benefits, you may qualify for financial assistance. This will enable you to get advice on the type of arguments that may be successful and whether the offer you are able to make is likely to be seen as reasonable by the Court. (See pages 111–112 for more information on Time Orders.) You will usually have to show that the current situation is temporary and that you will be able to resume payments after a set period.

A Time Order can change the terms of a credit agreement; the Court will consider the means of the debtor and any security in case of future default. Seek expert advice regarding what will be accepted by the Court as a reasonable offer when replying to the summons.

If threatened with repossession of goods on Hire Purchase or conditional sale agreements, contact the creditor in the first instance to try to prevent repossession by offering an acceptable and affordable repayment. If the creditor refuses your offer or is being unreasonable, you should reply to the summons and attend any Court Hearing or apply to the Court for a Time Order.

*K*ey points

- You must prioritise your debts in order to know how to deal with them.

- Be aware of the action that can be taken against you for non-payment (eg Court action, imprisonment or eviction).

- Prioritise housing debt to protect your home. Other priorities include utilities, fines and Council Tax.

- Negotiate a settlement with your priority creditors before you deal with your non-priority debts.

- Don't panic or ignore the situation – seek advice.

5 Negotiating with non-priority creditors

This chapter covers how to deal with non-priority debts. It sets out the four steps to take when negotiating with creditors, namely:

- *Contact your creditors and confirm the amount of debts*
- *Assess what resources you have available*
- *Examine your options*
- *Consider your creditors' possible responses and legal options*

It then looks in detail at how to choose and implement an appropriate option, giving examples and sample letters to illustrate the different situations.

Dealing with non-priority debts

The previous chapter looked at ways of stabilising priority debts. Attention now needs to be given to the non-priority debts; ie those debts where the sanction available to the creditor is less serious than for priority debts. In particular, in contrast with the priority debts outlined in Chapter 3, failure to pay non-priority debts will *not* mean the loss of housing, or essential utilities, nor, in any circumstances, imprisonment.

In earlier chapters we have gone through the first steps of identifying and obtaining details of non-priority creditors. The next step is to begin the process of negotiation.

Contact your creditors and confirm the amount of debts

Once you have obtained complete details of all your creditors, contact them, at first by letter, as in the example in Figure 1. **Always keep a copy of all correspondence with creditors.**

> Mr & Mrs Prescott
> 9 Station Road
> Roller Highway
> Runcorn RU1 2LP
>
> Dear Sir/Madam
>
> **Account Number 4545 123 456 789**
>
> We are currently experiencing financial difficulties and are anxious to try to resolve the problem and so we would be grateful if you would furnish us with the following details.
>
> 1 Whether the loan is secured? *(only ask this question if you don't know)*
> 2 Balance owed
> 3 Terms of repayment
> 4 Total arrears
> 5 Whether the interest is accruing and at what rate
> 6 Copy of the agreement *(only ask for this if you don't have a copy to hand)*
>
> Once all our creditors have replied we will contact you again with proposals for repayment. In the interim we ask that no further action is taken in this matter and that you stop any further interest or charges accruing on the account and confirm this in writing.
>
> Yours faithfully

Figure 1

This letter aims to achieve four things:

- it allows a breathing space to complete and check the viability of your Personal Budget;
- it ensures that an accurate balance and other details are obtained direct from creditors;
- it lets the creditors know what is happening; and
- it tries to stop the situation from getting worse by asking for interest and charges to be stopped.

It may take creditors a while to respond. You may need to write again to assure some creditors that matters are still in hand, as in Figure 2.

```
                                    Mr & Mrs Prescott
                                    9 Station Road
                                    Roller Highway
                                    Runcorn RU1 2LP

Dear Sir/Madam

Account Number 4545 123 456 789

Further to your letter of (insert date) providing us with
information about our account.

Unfortunately, not all creditors have replied as promptly
as you have, and we are not yet in a position to make
offers of repayment.

We have written again to those creditors who have not
replied and hope to contact you again in the near future
with an offer of repayment. In the meantime, we ask that
you continue to suspend enforcement action on this
account and confirm this in writing.

Thank you.

Yours faithfully
```

Figure 2

Once all your creditors have confirmed details of the debts, you should: assess your available resources; examine your options; and consider the creditors' responses and enforcement possibilities. Then you can move on to the implementation stage.

Assess what resources you have available

Your *Personal Budget* will provide basic income and expenditure information (see pages 27–29). You should also note any assets such as savings, shares and, where relevant, *equity* in the home. This provides a complete financial picture establishing both your disposable income and the assets that you have available to settle with the non-priority creditors.

During the time between first contact with your creditors and the point at which confirmation is received from all of them, you also have an opportunity to assess how satisfactorily your Personal Budget works.

Before contacting the creditors again, review your Personal Budget thoroughly and make any necessary adjustments. Then you can finalise your financial statement for presentation to your creditors. An example of how to set a financial statement out (Figure 3) is provided on the next page. A realistic *Personal Budget* is essential before you can examine options for settlement.

Examine your options

For any strategy to work, you must be committed to it. The objective is to negotiate a realistic settlement with your creditors. At the outset it is worthwhile defining 'realistic'. A realistic settlement of the debt means settling the debt in a shorter time than it would take to complete the most likely enforcement procedure. Normally this will be between two and three years, and sometimes up to five years. In some circumstances settlement may take place over a longer period, for example to avoid risk of repossession of the home. Overlong settlements need to be considered carefully and should be the exception rather than the rule.

The main options are detailed in the table on page 58.

Consider your creditors' possible responses and legal options

Before choosing your options, it is important to consider the possible objections of creditors. It is better to know and anticipate the likely reaction to your proposed strategy. Objections may include:

■ the cost of administering small payments;
■ objection to certain items or amounts of expenditure; and
■ company policy.

Income	£	p	Outgoings	£	p	Debt
Self			Rent (weekly × 52/12)			
Partner (net – ie after tax)			Mortgage			
Other (net)			Council Tax			
Income Support			Housekeeping			
Disability Living Allowance			Insurance			
Pension (Work)			Electricity			
(State)			Other fuel			
			Car/Travel			
			Water			
			TV licence			
			Phone (quarter × 4/12)			
			Prescriptions			
			Clothing			
			Care costs			
TOTAL			TOTAL			

Figure 3

57

Option	Usual financial context	Main purpose
Moratorium on the debt	No disposable income for a time, but prospect of reasonable improvement in near future.	To get a breathing space of 3 or more months to see if circumstances change for the better. May be followed by write off.
Write off debt	No funds, or no cost-effective realisable assets available now or in the foreseeable future.	To obtain permanent discharge of debts.
Partially write off debt	Some funds are available to pay towards debt, with the remainder being written off.	Bringing a settlement proposal within a realistic timescale, which would avoid bankruptcy.
Selling non-essential assets	Little or no disposable income.	Fully settling debt, or contributing to partial write off.
Token offer	Only small amount available after income and expenditure stabilised.	Breathing space – as in moratorium. Could be pending improvement or could be followed by write off, where situation unlikely to change for better.
Rescheduling	Reasonable disposable income and debts payable within a reasonable time.	Settling debts by pro rata instalments to creditors.
Refinancing	Required repayments comfortably below disposable income level.	To fully settle debts or provide the means to settle at a discounted lump-sum rate.
Administration Order	Some disposable income and total debts not exceeding £5,000. Once Court Judgment against you.	Settlement of debts via Court administration.
Individual Voluntary Arrangement (IVA)	Substantial disposable income and/or realisable assets to make creditors a reasonable offer. May also need to have funds to pay administration fee of about £1,500–£3,000.	Settlement of debts via agreed plan under supervision of private administrator, over 3 to 5 years for example.
Bankruptcy	Insolvent but can find petition fee of £370.	Discharge of debts by court-appointed administrator.

▼

The Brown Chip Card Company objects to **Mr Desmond King** spending £200 on car transport and wants the car sold and the sale proceeds applied to its account. It could appropriately be pointed out that one or a combination of the following reasons make this an unrealistic suggestion:

■ Mr King needs the car for work, at times/locations when there is no reasonably available public transport;

■ Mr King or a member of his household is disabled and requires the car to meet mobility or medical needs;

■ the costs involved in not having access to a car are greater than the savings to be made; or

■ any savings made must be distributed fairly between all creditors.

Some of the objections can be easily addressed. For example, as long as the expenditure headings are reasonable, it is rare to get objections on this point. If a creditor does object, then be prepared to justify your position.

Other objections can be overcome by offering practical solutions – for example administration costs can be minimised by extending payment periods from monthly to quarterly in appropriate circumstances. Some objections need to be dealt with by a more senior figure if they relate to company policy; in these cases the first contact may not be able to agree matters beyond certain limits.

You will also need to consider what legal sanctions are available to the creditor. What if the creditor chooses to enforce the debt via Court action? (Chapter 6 deals in detail with Court procedure.) You need to think about the Court system itself as a backdrop to negotiation. What would be the likely consequences of Court action being taken against you? Make sure that you get proper advice about this before agreeing anything with creditors.

You need also to differentiate between single and multiple debts. This is because:

- For single debts there is the possibility of an *Instalment Order* – this means that the Court will determine the rate of payment and in doing so will take into account your statement of means when calculating your Instalment Order.
- For multiple debts of under £5,000 in total, payment by instalments is a possible option, by means of an application for an *Administration Order* (see pages 104–111).
- For multiple debts of over £5,000 in total, you will need to rely on a negotiated settlement.

It is important to bear in mind that the Court is interested in what you can reasonably afford to pay. Once a County Court Judgment is made, interest will normally be frozen. The Court also takes into account your personal and financial circumstances in setting levels of payment. It is also concerned that creditors obtain a proportionate share of available funds based on the respective balances owed. This is known as a 'pro rata' or 'equitable distribution' (see page 68 for an example of how a pro rata calculation works).

Implementation

Implementation of an agreement includes the following elements:

- Choose an appropriate option
- Presentation
- Deal with objections
- Payment closure

Choose an appropriate option

There are no absolute rules about how to negotiate with creditors. However, in general your options can be split into three types:

Informal A – where you have little or no money
Informal B – where you have funds
Legal – with or without funds

In the table on page 58, the main purpose of each option and the relevant financial circumstances were listed. You may want to look back at this table before reading on.

In the next section we will consider each option in turn by examining its practical implementation.

Informal (A) approach, if you have no money or very little

Les and Pat Smith owe their various creditors around £3,000. Problems started when Les, who is 62, retired due to ill health on a reduced occupational pension. Pat, who is 61, works for a company which has a retirement age of 65 for both sexes. She has been granted compassionate leave to look after him in the meantime. Their combined income just about meets their normal expenditure, but there is nothing spare to pay creditors. Les' small retirement lump sum was used to pay off rent arrears.

Pat reckons that she will be back at work in around three months' time. Her salary will be enough to at least resume normal payments. A moratorium seems the most suitable option, as the problem is likely to be temporary and has a reasonable (although not guaranteed) prospect of being improved. Les and Pat's creditors are sent the letter (Figure 4) on page 62.

A moratorium allows some breathing space, but creditors will come back at some later point (usually three to six months) and request an update. It is important that once you have been given a time when you are likely to hear from the creditors that you make a note of it and make sure that you give them an up-to-date picture of your situation at the time.

If objections are lodged by the creditor, you can try to counter them by reference to:

```
                                        Les & Pat Smith
                                     29 Inkerman Street
                                      Salford AB1 2CD

Dear Sir/Madam

Account Number 555435 767 890

Further to our recent letter, we enclose a copy of our
financial statement.

We are experiencing temporary financial difficulties due
to Les' illness and the need for Pat to provide full-time
care for the time being. Pat expects to be making a
return to work once matters have stabilised. Current med-
ical opinion is that she should be able to resume work in
three to four months' time.

As you can see from the financial statement, after meet-
ing essential expenditure there is no available income
with which to make an offer to creditors. We would there-
fore ask for a moratorium on our account, for the time
being. We look forward to your positive reply.

Yours faithfully
```

Figure 4 Moratorium

- the realities of the situation as contained in the financial statement;
- other creditors who have already agreed; and
- the fact that any enforcement measure will only make things worse, without necessarily benefitting either party because you haven't any available income.

A variation on this option may be a token offer – for example 50 pence per month to each creditor – symbolising a commitment but not the means to pay (Figure 5).

Les & Pat Smith
29 Inkerman Street
Salford AB1 2CD

Dear Sir/Madam

Account Number 555435 767 890

Further to our recent letter, we enclose a copy of our
financial statement.

We are experiencing financial difficulties because …

As you can see, after meeting essential expenditure,
there is no available income with which to make an offer.
However, we can make a token payment of [50 pence] per
month to you.

We request that you freeze the account for the time
being. We will contact you as our circumstances improve.
We look forward to your positive reply.

Yours faithfully

Figure 5 Token offer

A request to totally and finally *write off* the debt would be appropriate where the situation was identified as irrecoverable, for
example if Pat was now suffering long-term stress-related illness
(Figure 6).

```
                                          Les & Pat Smith
                                       29 Inkerman Street
                                        Salford AB1 2CD

Dear Sir/Madam

Account Number 555435 767 890

Further to our recent letter, we enclose a copy of our
financial statement.

*We are experiencing financial difficulties because …
.*/*Our situation has not changed since we last wrote to
you on … *

As you can see, after meeting essential expenditure,
there is no available income with which to make an offer.
We request that you *write the account off*/*grant a fur-
ther moratorium of …*, as the situation is unlikely to
improve in the foreseeable future.

We look forward to your positive reply.

Yours faithfully

(Delete * as appropriate)
```

Figure 6 Write off

Informal (B) approach, if you have funds

Three months later, Les has recovered well enough for Pat to
return to work. They have reviewed their situation and have a disposable income of £25 per month. The situation is unlikely to
change in the future. It will take at least ten years to pay off the
£3,000. Over three years, Pat could manage £900. A partial write
off may help ease the situation and allow payment within a reasonable timescale. What is reasonable will depend on the
seriousness and stability of the overall situation. The more serious
and less stable situations should be settled within a maximum of
three years. Five years should be the target in all other cases. The
letter below (Figure 7) should be suitable:

Les & Pat Smith
29 Inkerman Street
Salford AB1 2CD

Dear Sir/Madam

Account Number 555435 767 890

We refer to previous correspondence on the above account. We enclose a financial statement. From this you will see that the offer proposed is small. You are of course aware from our previous correspondence that our situation is unlikely to change in the future.

In order to facilitate a reasonable settlement of our indebtedness, we would ask you to write off 70% of the outstanding balance. In the circumstances this represents our best effort and a reasonable target for settlement. *The alternative would be to seek an Administration Order. This may obtain a similar result, but would involve extra cost and therefore reduced recovery.**

We would ask for your positive consideration of the proposal and look forward to hearing from you in the near future.

Yours faithfully

(*Optional if circumstances suit at the time, or may use similar phrasing in reply to rejection of the offer.)

Figure 7 Partial write-off

If Les and Pat had no disposable income, but their cousin Fred was willing to pay a £900 lump sum, then a modified version of the above letter could be used. Alternatively a full and final settlement letter as below (Figure 8) could be used to all creditors. Again, reference to an Administration Order may be made if appropriate or in reply to a rejection (see page 104).

Going back to our earlier scenario, let us assume that Fred couldn't help and Pat can't return to work. However Pat receives a retirement lump sum from her former employer. If the lump sum is greater than the debts, then this could be offered in full settlement. Where it is

> Les & Pat Smith
> 29 Inkerman Street
> Salford AB1 2CD
>
> Dear Sir/Madam
>
> **Account Number 555435 767 890**
>
> We refer to previous correspondence on the above. We enclose a financial statement from which you will see that there is no spare income for offers to be made to creditors and we cannot see any improvement in the fore-seeable future.
>
> We do have a lump sum of £900 from a family member that we propose to offer proportionally, in full and final settlement of our debts. Having reviewed our income and expenditure we feel that this course of action is the best available solution to help us make at least some contribution to our debts.
>
> As you will be aware, such an approach will depend upon all our creditors accepting the offer and we look forward to your positive response in due course.
>
> Yours faithfully

Figure 8 Full and final settlement offer

less than the total debts, it could provide the funds for an offer of part of the debts with a partial write off.

Another option here would be selling non-essential assets. This might include a piece of jewellery for example. You need to carefully examine all the implications of selling non-essential assets. As a minimum you need to establish that the assets are:

- genuinely non-essential;
- not already seized by a bailiff for one of your debts;
- properly valued; and
- fairly realised.

Establishing if the asset is non-essential is straightforward. By definition, an asset *is* essential if it is:

- secured or attached to your home;
- a vital utility, required for work;
- a source of income generation; or
- required for someone's health.

Valuing and selling assets often requires referral to a reliable expert. The expert could be anyone from an independent financial adviser to an antiques dealer. If a reliable contact is not known, then always get the opinion of more than one expert.

Income		£
Wages		529.93
Occupational pension		110.00
	Total	**639.93**
Expenditure		**£**
Rent		58.50
Council Tax		17.98
TV rental		20.00
Housekeeping		180.00
Insurance		6.92
Electricity		41.54
Gas		63.40
Car		206.31
TV licence		9.23
Telephone		26.09
Clothing		12.00
Water charge		5.09
	Total balance	**647.06**
	Shortfall	**7.13**

Figure 9 Les and Pat's monthly financial statement

After an initial moratorium, Les and Pat's situation improves from the statement shown at Figure 9.

Les is awarded a higher rate of the mobility component of Disability Living Allowance (see page 25) due to his severe disability. This helps towards running the car. The backdated amount is spent on urgent repairs. The extra £155.35 per month increases the amount available for creditors to £148.22. This can be offered to the creditors on a pro rata basis and clears the debts off in just under two years.

A pro rata reschedule of the available income is a fair and reasonable way of distributing funds. It is also the method used by the Court in Administration Orders. Creditors are used to, and are usually prepared to accept, this approach.

Here is a simple example of how a pro rata calculation works:

Frank Black has the following circumstances.

His weekly income is £100.

His weekly expenditure is £80. His weekly surplus is therefore £20. The amount he owes to each creditor is as follows:

Swift Loan Company Ltd	£200
Catalogue Shop	£150
Major Carpets	£200
Total amount owed	£550

The amount due each creditor can be calculated as follows:

Multiply the weekly surplus × the individual debt and divide by the total debt

Swift Loan would get	$20 \times 200 \div 550 = £7.28$ per week
Catalogue Shop would get	$20 \times 150 \div 550 = £5.45$ per week
Major Carpets would get	$20 \times 200 \div 550 = £7.27$ per week

Total = £20 (£7.28 + £5.45 + £7.27)

Les and Pat's circumstances are set out in the revised financial statement (Figure 11) and their creditors are listed on the repayment schedule (Figure 12). They enclose both with a covering letter, an example of which is given below (Figure 10).

Les & Pat Smith
29 Inkerman Street
Salford AB1 2CD

Dear Sir/Madam

Account Number 555435 767 890

Further to our letter of *(insert date)*, in which our circumstances were outlined, we now enclose a copy of our financial statement.

As you can see, after meeting essential expenditure there is some available income which is offered on a **pro rata** basis.

We ask that you accept the offer and stop the interest accruing on this account in order that the payments will begin to reduce the debt.

Please send us a paying in book so that we can ensure regular payments.**

If the offer is not acceptable, we would be obliged if you could explain your reasons.

We look forward to your positive reply.

Yours faithfully

(*See page 72 re interest stopping and insert if required)

(**Insert if required for the appropriate period)

Figure 10 Pro rata offer

Income	£	
Wages	529.93	
Occupational pension	110.00	
Disability Living Allowance	155.35	
Total	**795.28**	
Expenditure	**£**	
Rent	58.50	
Council Tax	17.98	
TV rental	20.00	
Housekeeping	180.00	
Insurance	6.92	
Electricity	41.54	
Gas	63.40	
Car	206.31	
TV licence	9.23	
Telephone	26.09	
Clothing	12.00	
Water charge	5.09	
Total balance	**647.06**	
Total disposable income	**148.22**	

Figure 11 Revised monthly financial statement

Creditor payments	Outstanding balance	Proposed monthly payments
Wanset Bank	1439.86	64.17
Wanamakers	962.55	42.89
DECRATS	386.07	17.20
Leangoods	298.12	13.29
Severeds	257.00	11.45
TOTALS	3343.60	149.00
Monthly amount available:		**£149.00**

Figure 12 Repayment schedule

If your offer is relatively small, and therefore may be unattractive to the creditor, it may be worth amending the letter as follows (Figure 13):

Les & Pat Smith
29 Inkerman Street
Salford AB1 2CD

Dear Sir/Madam

Account number 555435 767 890

Following our previous correspondence and further discussions with a member of your staff on the telephone we now enclose a statement showing our financial position. Also enclosed is a repayment proposal showing how the balance of income is to be distributed.

Whilst we appreciate that the offer of £00 per week is small, we feel that it is realistic in the circumstances and do hope that this will be accepted by yourselves as an alternative to legal recovery procedures and subsequent costs. May we stress that to enable us to maintain the proposed schedule of repayments it will be necessary to obtain the agreement of all creditors.

We would ask whether you will consider foregoing further interest charges in order to assist us to pay off the capital sum owed.

Your co-operation is appreciated and we look forward to receiving your written agreement.

Yours faithfully

Figure 13

The offer letter (Figure 10) asks for interest to cease accruing on the account. This is very important where the interest is added on a running account basis (see page 20). Credit and store cards are an example of such accounts. Check carefully, however, as some instalment creditors have interest running on the same basis.

The reason for stopping interest is that accruing charges will seriously hinder the reduction of the debt within a reasonable time. In some cases it will increase the debt even if you are making payments.

If you cannot afford the contractual payments, accumulating interest merely serves to aggravate the situation. Stopping charges and interest at the outset helps to establish a stable basis for assessing the situation.

If some creditors have agreed to freeze interest, but others are proving reluctant to join in, it may be worth another letter, as in Figure 14.

```
                                        Les & Pat Smith
                                    29 Inkerman Street
                                      Salford AB1 2CD

Dear Sir/Madam

Account number 555435 767 890

Thank you for your recent letter accepting our offer of
repayment. We are disappointed to see that you have not
agreed to stop the interest on the account. As you will
appreciate, if the interest is not stopped then the bal-
ance on the account will continue to rise and we will
never be able to repay the debt.

We would ask that you reconsider your decision on this
case and advise us in writing accordingly.

Yours faithfully
```

Figure 14

There are some situations where interest will not normally be stopped, for example where the offered payments exceed the amount of interest owing. If a creditor is reluctant to stop interest, you can try pointing out that:

■ Other creditors who have accepted the offer would be unfairly disadvantaged.

- If pursued through the Court, it is unlikely that the creditor would be entitled to interest.

Where a pro rata offer is being rejected in its entirety ask the creditor why. Otherwise, in general terms, use similar justifications for asking the creditor to reconsider, ie:

- Other creditors who have accepted the offer would be unfairly disadvantaged.
- If pursued through the Court, it is precisely how an *Administration Order* is paid and the concept is generally accepted by the courts.

Payments

Calculating the rescheduled offer (in Figure 12) is fairly straightforward. The total payment amount is divided by the total debt and then multiplied by each individual debt to give each creditor's pro rata share. Check the results by adding up all the individual payments; they should equal the total monthly payment.

It should be clear from the financial statement that the offer is realistic in the circumstances and that all creditors are being treated fairly.

There are three golden rules regarding actual payment:

1 The payment method should be suitable for your circumstances.
2 The payment method should be as low cost as possible.
3 The frequency of payments should fall in line if possible with your own budget period. Don't, for example, offer to pay on a four-weekly basis if you get paid or receive benefit or pension on a calendar month basis.

Each repayment to an individual creditor should begin on the first payment period after acceptance has been received. However, if no formal acceptance is received within one month, for example, it is usually advisable to start paying anyway, and to write to the creditor again asking for a reply.

A summary of payment methods is given in the table overleaf:

Payment method	Details
Bank Standing Order	Normally monthly payments. Where the bank is a creditor, it may be useful to get them onside in administering payments.
Bank Direct Debit	Same as above, except only do it if there are few creditors, or the bank is willing to make the arrangements. Otherwise the setting up is difficult and time consuming.
Cheque	Fairly simple and easy, subject to postal security. You also need to consider possible charges and monitoring account/overdraft limits. Affordability depends on charges.
Post Office Giro Bank payment books	Some creditors subsidise payments via post office giro, or payment book arrangements via some banks. The giro system is expensive if unsubsidised (about 85p per payment at the time of writing). It may, however, be the most suitable method for people who do not have bank accounts.
Postal Order	Tends to be the most expensive method. Unfortunately for many people without bank accounts, it is the only method available.
In person	Suitable if a creditor has a local office or collection point. May, however, be a source of pressure for increased payments.
Client account	Probably the best solution of all. Access unfortunately very limited. Only a few traditional money advice services provide this facility in the form of Paylink. Consumer Credit Counselling Service (see page 8), private debt adjustment agencies and (in the context of IVAs) insolvency practitioners, may provide this facility.

(Adapted with permission from *A Guide to Money Advice in Scotland* – Gray, Benison and Gallacher. Money Advice Trust, 1997)

Where there are a large number of creditors and the only available method is costly, consider including the cost in your Personal Budget and reducing offers accordingly.

Refinancing as an option

This involves consolidating (combining) your debts into one loan, usually secured against property. Refinancing is usually only a complete solution in the following circumstances:

- when the amount borrowed is equal to the debts owed; and
- any repayments are confortably affordable.

Refinancing debts, particularly into a secured loan, is usually a last resort and specialist help is very important. You must have access to a reliable independent financial adviser and/or a solicitor. You should make sure that you understand the nature of the transaction, and in particular that you are swapping unsecured for secured debt. If the security is the equity in your house (the equity in a home is the value left after deduction of any current securities, such as a mortgage and/or second mortgage), then you must consider the risk of repossession in the event of non-payment or breach of agreement.

The objectives in refinancing can include:

- making a full settlement;
- funding a lump sum for partial write off; or
- reducing current expenditure or debts.

Although current expenditure may be reduced, the payments will usually be made over a lengthy period and the overall cost may be higher in the long term.

There are three main methods of refinancing:

- finding a suitable loan product on the market;
- creating a voluntary charge (see below) in favour of creditors; or
- selling up and moving on.

None of these may appear particularly attractive, but in certain circumstances they may provide the only viable choice. Which method you use depends on several factors:

- family circumstance;
- age;
- equity available;
- disposable income; and
- the sanctions you wish to avoid.

The circumstances which might encourage you to consider these options are when the asset itself may be under threat or when very serious sanctions are threatened (eg you are facing *committal* proceedings for Council Tax debts).

Loan products

Some of the available financial products are listed in the table below. The services of a reliable independent financial adviser (IFA) are essential. A friend or relative may be able to recommend one they have used themselves. Otherwise you can find one through *Yellow Pages* or by contacting IFA Promotion Ltd or the Financial Services Authority at the addresses on page 164. The FSA will not be able to recommend a particular firm or individual but it will be able to tell you if there is an IFA in your area.

Product type	Basic financial requirements
Loan secured on insurance policy	You need an appropriate policy (eg non-house purchase endowment). Payments must be comfortably within your budget.
Remortgage	Sufficient equity to enable clearance of balances outstanding, or lump-sum full and final proportional settlement.
Second mortgage	As for remortgage. Suitable if shorter loan term feasible. Not for the unwary – try and avoid non-status sector (ie those who lend to people with no credit history and often charge higher rates of interest than the high street providers).
Equity release or maturity loans	Large amount of equity, and ability to meet interest payments if required. Some agreements allow you lifetime residence and obtain repayment on sale of property, or death of borrower (see page 26).

Voluntary charge

If you have a lot of equity in your property, some creditors may agree to accept a *voluntary charge* from you to secure their debt. Always seek advice to see if this is an advisable option. You must also get legal advice about the terms and conditions of the mortgage itself. This advice may be expensive but is essential to ensure that you are not unduly disadvantaged by the agreement. The voluntary charge can be conditional on instalments, interest only, or realisable (repaid) only in the event of the debtor selling the property. It can also be conditional on no further interest accruing.

Selling up

Selling non-essential assets has been dealt with above (see page 66). The sale of your home to realise equity to pay unsecured debt has more serious consequences. It is the least desirable option and is only worthwhile if:

- you are able to find suitable alternative accommodation; and
- it will release enough equity to make a significant impact on your debts.

The amount of equity released needs to be sufficient to pay all the debts, or allow a reasonable *full and final settlement* with creditors.

If moving to a smaller, cheaper property is not possible, you may need to make a request for rehousing via the local authority or a housing association. The housing body concerned may try to say that you have made yourself intentionally homeless. However, the code of practice on homelessness states that people should not be treated as intentionally homeless if their house was sold due to real financial difficulties.

Legal, with or without funds

Administration Orders

You may wish to consider an *Administration Order*, if your total debts do not exceed £5,000 and you have a Court Judgment registered against you. The Court administers payments to all the creditors included in the Order and interest is stopped. Whilst it is in operation, creditors cannot take any enforcement action against you without the permission of the Court.

For detailed information about *Administration Orders* see pages 104–111 in Chapter 6.

Bankruptcy

Bankruptcy procedures involve the appointment of a supervisor (known as a 'trustee') to administer your affairs. The trustee's main task is to sell your assets for the benefit of the creditors. You can make yourself bankrupt or a creditor may do so.

Formal bankruptcy is most appropriate for someone who:

- has large debts which can't be paid off;
- has little or no assets;
- is not a homeowner; and
- has a low income.

Bankruptcy can affect your housing, employment status and credit rating. Detailed information about bankruptcy is given in Chapter 7.

Combination of options

The options discussed in this chapter can be used on their own or in combination. One example is to request *write off* or partial write off, in order to reduce the overall balance of your debts to under £5,000 to facilitate an *Administration Order*. Whichever option or combination you use, the prime consideration is that you find one which suits you. If you are not sure about anything, seek advice, as explained in Chapter 1.

*K*ey points

- Contact your creditors and confirm how much you owe.

- Check what resources you have to offer in settlement of your debts.

- Look at all your options.

- Consider what your creditors are saying – is there room for a negotiated settlement of your problems?

- Draw up a proposal and send it to your creditors (examples are given to show how to do this).

- Try to get their agreement to your proposal.

- If at first you don't succeed, try again and again.

6 The County Court

This chapter covers:

- *What is the County Court?*
- *What happens if an unsecured creditor takes you to the County Court?*
- *Paying County Court Judgments*
- *Enforcement of County Court Judgments*
- *How to set aside a County Court Judgment*
- *County Court fees*
- *Administration Orders*
- *Time Orders*

What is the County Court?

The County Court is the Court where all civil matters are dealt with – this includes divorce, child access and issues relating to most debts. It is important to remember that the County Court is a civil court, *not* a criminal court.

Creditors use the County Court when people owe them money. The particular matters dealt with by the County Court and relevant to this book are:

- where you owe money on a credit debt (eg a credit card) and have not kept up with the payments and you cannot come to an arrangement with the creditor; or
- where you have bought an item on Hire Purchase that the creditor wants returned because you have fallen behind with the contractual payment or you cannot agree with the creditor how to repay the debt.

You can often make your own applications to the County Court to assist with any debt problems that you have, for example for *Administration Orders* or *Time Orders* (see below).

80

What happens if an unsecured creditor takes you to the County Court?

If an unsecured creditor decides to take action against you for the recovery of money in the County Court, they will ask the Court to issue a Claim Form (see sample on pages 143–144). This form states that the creditor (they are called the 'claimant' on the form) is owed money by you (the Court uses the word 'defendant').

When the creditor issues the paperwork to the Court they have to include a summary of how much you borrowed and what has happened (eg failure to maintain payments) to make them take action against you – this is called the 'Particulars of Claim'. They should also attach a copy of any written agreement (eg consumer credit agreement) *unless* the paperwork has been issued by a 'Central Production Centre'. If you are finding it difficult to understand which Court to respond to, contact an advice agency, or the Court that issued the claim form, for clarification.

If you receive a Claim Form, you have to reply to it within a certain time limit, as explained below. The Court decides how much you owe and at what rate it should be paid back to the creditor. It will take into account your ability to pay but only if you tell the Court your circumstances. Otherwise the Court will usually give the creditor the order they have requested. It is therefore very important that you reply to the *Claim*. If you do not reply the Court will not have enough information to make a fair decision, and is likely to order you to pay the debt in full immediately.

If you are struggling to complete the form, seek advice from one of the agencies listed in Chapter 1.

Remember that just because a creditor is taking Court action, that does not make them a priority creditor. The amount of any payment offer should be calculated according to the principles already explained. How you reply to the Claim will depend on whether you:

- agree that you owe all the money:
- agree that you owe some of the money (called 'partially admitting the debt'); or
- do not think that you owe any of the money (called 'disputing the debt').

Forms will be included with the claim form which correspond to each of the above options. You need to fill in the appropriate form and return it to the Court, or to the creditor, within the specified timescale shown in the papers.

If you agree that you owe the total amount

If this is the case, you need to complete the 'Admission Form' (called form **N9A**). On the first side of the form it asks:

- personal details such as your date of birth and employment status;
- who else (if anyone) lives with you; and
- whether you own your property or rent it.

The other side of the form asks for details of your income and expenditure (similar to a Personal Budget) and priority and non-priority debts. If the creditor rejects your offer, the Court will use this information to decide how much you should pay.

If you have already completed a Personal Budget (see pages 27–29) and worked out repayments to your priority and non-priority creditors, it will be easy for you to transfer the information onto the form. If your budget includes expenditure which is not listed on the Court form – for example, prescriptions – then put these in the 'other items' section of the form.

When working out your offer of repayment, refer back to Chapter 5 on negotiating with creditors. You should put your offer of repayment in the bottom right-hand box of the form.

Once you have completed the Admission Form, you must return it to the creditor at the address shown on the claim. If different addresses appear on the front and back of the form, check with the creditor which address to use. The form must be returned within 16 days of the date of the delivery postmark. Make sure that you keep a copy of the form and send it by recorded delivery if possible.

Once your creditor receives the form, they will decide whether or not they agree to your offer of repayment. If they agree, they will notify the Court and ask for a Judgment in the terms of your offer. The Court staff will then send a copy of the Judgment out to you confirming how much you have to pay each week or month and the date by which the first payment has to be made. How to pay your County Court Judgment is explained later in this Chapter on pages 90–92.

If the creditor does not agree with the repayment offer that you have made, they will send your Admission Form to the Court and tell them. The Court will then decide how much you should pay:

- If your debt is less than £50,000 an initial decision is made by Court staff.
- If you owe more than £50,000 it is done by a District Judge.

A Judgment will be sent out to you by post detailing the terms that the Court has decided. If you do not agree with the decision on repayment terms you need to apply for a 'Redetermination'. This must be done within 14 days of getting the Judgment. To do this you need to complete a County Court form, called an **N244**, which you can collect from your local County Court. (A sample N244 is shown on pages 151–153.) Alternatively, your Court may accept a letter from you. In either case, there is no fee.

In either the **N244** or a letter you need to explain why you want the decision to be looked at again; for example because you cannot afford the repayments the Court has ordered. You should also include details of your income and expenditure. These will probably be the figures that you put on the **N9A** (Admission Form).

Redetermination is always decided by a District Judge. If Court staff made the original decision, the District Judge may just look at the papers again or they could arrange for a Hearing. If the original decision was made by a District Judge, then there has to be a Hearing.

If there is a Hearing, it will be held at your local County Court. It will be held in the District Judge's office and you must attend. The creditor may also attend. Take your copy of the reply form with you and also a copy of your *Personal Budget*. You will get the opportunity to explain to the District Judge why you are asking for the decision to be changed. For example, you may need to ask the Court to take into account expenditure which they had previously ignored.

If you dispute the whole debt

Before you decide to dispute a debt you should consider getting advice from an advice agency as they will be able to give you some indication of whether or not you have a valid defence and the chances of it being successful.

If you do not agree that you owe any of the debt, you need to do one of two things. Either:

- complete the 'Defence Form' (**N9B**); or
- complete the 'Acknowledgement of Service Form' (**N9**).

If you feel confident that you can explain why you dispute the debt without providing any further supporting information, then you can just fill in the Defence Form (as explained below), which you must return to the Court within 16 days. Don't forget to keep a copy.

If you are going to need extra time to complete the Defence Form, you should return the Acknowledgement of Service Form, first ticking the box that says that you wish to dispute the debt. This form must be returned to the Court within 16 days. If you have done this, you then have another 14 days to return your Defence Form.

Filling in a Defence Form

When you fill in a Defence Form, you need to explain on it *why* you dispute the debt – simply denying that you owe the debt without giving reasons will not be sufficient. Reasons for disputing the debt may include:

- that you paid the debt off before the claim was issued; or
- that you dispute that you are liable for the debt.

You will also need to complete the 'Statement of Truth' which is included in the form. This is a statement saying that you believe what you have said to be true. The Court requires you to do this so that you cannot change your arguments as to why you do not owe the money at a later date.

Once the Court has received your Defence Form they will process the papers, which will be given a reference number and will now be known as a 'case'. The case will be named as follows: Creditor–v–You.

Both sides will then be sent an allocation questionnaire to complete and return to the Court. This will help the Court decide to which 'track' the case should be allocated. The County Court deals with claims for money by allocating them to certain 'tracks'. The procedure which follows will depend on the track allocated. Most credit debts will be dealt with under the *Small Claims* Track, as the cases are not usually complicated. There are three tracks:

- Small Claims Track
- Fast Track
- Multi Track

The track chosen by the Court will depend on a number of factors:

- **The size of the debt** – If the case appears straightforward, this will be the main criteria. The general rule is that if the debt is £5,000 or less it will be allocated to Small Claims; if it is between £5,000 and £15,000 it will be Fast Track; and if it is above £15,000 it will be Multi Track. However, other factors can alter this.
- **The complexity of the case** – the Court will assess how long the case is likely to take, whether there will be a great deal of evidence to consider, and whether complicated issues are involved.
- **The circumstances of the parties involved** – if one of the parties is not working, for example, and has little income to pay for legal

advice, this may mean that the Court will choose the Small Claims Track regardless of the size of the debt.

- **Whether the decision that the Court will make is likely to have an effect on many other people** – ie the legal ruling in the case (the 'precedent') would be considered by Courts in deciding future similar cases.
- **Whether expert witnesses will be needed**.

Even if a debt is more than £5,000, where both parties agree and the Court thinks that it is appropriate, the case can be allocated to the Small Claims Track.

If a case is allocated to one track and it later proves that a different track would have been more appropriate, the Court can change the allocation.

Small Claims procedure

If the Court allocates your case to the Small Claims Track, it believes that the matter can be dealt with quickly and simply.

The Court will send a 'Notice of Allocation', which will tell you how the case is to proceed. Which form you receive will depend on the following:

- **N157** – will be sent if the Court is to give usual instructions (called 'Directions') and there needs to be a Hearing.
- **N160** – will be sent if more than £5,000 is owed but both parties have agreed to use Small Claims.
- **N159** – will be sent if the Court thinks that a decision can be made without a Hearing.
- **N158** – will be sent if the Court thinks that there should be a Preliminary Hearing before the full Hearing.

Each form will have 'Directions' attached to it. Standard Directions will normally order each side to send each other the documents that they intend to use at the Hearing. Special Directions will be used when the Court has specific requirements of either one or both of the parties.

The Court may order a Preliminary Hearing. This is likely when the Judge thinks that you have no chance of successfully disputing the debt or because they wish to issue special Directions. You must attend this Hearing.

If your case is to proceed, the next stage will be the full Hearing. You will have 21 days notice of the date of the Hearing. The notice will also indicate how long the Court expects the Hearing to last.

At the Hearing you can represent yourself or you can have a 'Lay Adviser' represent you. The Hearing is normally held in public but is relatively informal. You are not required to give evidence on oath and the Judge can conduct the proceedings as they see fit. At the end of the Hearing, the Judge will make a decision and briefly explain the reasons for it.

Fast Track

If your case is allocated to this track, you will be notified on the form **N154**. The form will also include Directions, a date for 'trial' (the Hearing) and a 'Listing Questionnaire' (**N170**).

The Directions will be a timetable of when each stage of the process will happen. In addition to the trial date, there will also be dates for returning the Listing Questionnaire, for 'disclosure', and for exchanging documents. Disclosure means that the two parties will have to show each other the evidence that they intend to rely on in Court.

The Listing Questionnaire (**N170**) asks each party:

- whether they have complied with the Directions;
- to confirm what issues they believe remain outstanding; and
- to estimate how long the Hearing will take.

Before the Hearing the Judge may send further Directions to either party.

The Hearing is normally held in public and is more formal than the Small Claims process. However it should take no more than one day. You will be on oath and you will not be able to use a Lay Adviser, so unless you can pay for a solicitor your only option will be to use a 'McKenzie Friend' with the Court's permission. A McKenzie Friend is someone who can accompany you to the Hearing and help you present your case but they cannot speak on your behalf.

At the end of the Hearing the District Judge will give their decision and provide brief reasons for it.

Multi Track

There is no standard procedure for Multi Track claims. The Court will manage this according to the needs of the case. The Court will, however, always give the date of the 'Case Management Conference' at which you and the other side would be given Directions and asked to agree what issues the claim was about. The Case Management Conference also establishes a timescale for how the case will proceed. The Court may send a Listing Questionnaire (**N170**) as with the Fast Track process above.

Once the Court receives the Listing Questionnaire, your case may go to 'Pre Trial Review'. This is a meeting held in private where you and the creditor will be encouraged to settle the matter without going to full trial (and thus avoiding costs). If you can't agree, or if there is no Pre Trial Review, the Hearing is normally held in public and is more formal than the Small Claims process. However it should take no more than one day. You will be on oath and you will not be able to use a Lay Adviser, so unless you can pay for a solicitor your only option will be to use a McKenzie Friend with the Court's permission. As with Fast Track, this means that someone can accompany you to the Hearing and help you present your case but they cannot speak on your behalf.

If you decide to dispute a debt you *must* attend all the Hearings and you *must* return all the paperwork that the Court sends. **You should also be aware that if you lose you may be responsible for the other side's costs**.

If you admit part of the debt

If you think that you owe part of the debt but not all of it, you need to complete both the Admission Form (N9A) and the Defence Form (N9B) following the explanations in the sections above. You should send both forms back to the Court.

Hire Purchase

If you have paid more than a third of the total amount on a Hire Purchase agreement, and the creditor wishes to try and repossess the item because you are in arrears, then they will have to do so through the County Court. The Court will issue a claim that will have details of when a Hearing will take place. The creditor will have to send 'Particulars of Claim' giving details of your agreement and details of the payments you have missed. If you have a defence, you do not have to complete a Defence Form, although it is advisable to. You must however attend the Hearing if you wish to dispute the debt.

If you wish to keep the item, you need to complete the Form of Admission (**N9C**), making an offer of payment. You should then send this form to the County Court.

The Court will send the form to the creditor and if the creditor accepts your terms of repayment, there will *not* normally be a Hearing. If the creditor accepts the offer, the Court will make a Suspended Return of Goods Order. This means that, providing you maintain the payments, the creditor has agreed that the item will not be repossessed.

It is very important at this stage that you decide whether or not you want or can afford to keep the item that is on Hire Purchase. This is because whether the item is repossessed or whether you voluntarily return it affects how any remaining balance is calculated after the item has been sold. You will normally owe less if you voluntarily return the item.

If the creditor does not accept the offer of repayment, there will be a Hearing at your local County Court.

If the item is a car and you cannot afford the normal monthly instalment but can make a reduced offer, and you need the car either because of mobility problems or for work, the District Judge may agree that you can pay a reduced monthly instalment (in effect a Time Order – see pages 111–112). Normally, however, the Court will expect you to offer the monthly instalment plus an amount towards the arrears. As Hire Purchase arrears are a priority debt, you will be able to work out from your Personal Budget how much you can afford to pay towards your arrears.

When you attend the Hearing, try to speak to the representative of the creditor before you go into the District Judge's office. You may be able to agree your offer of repayment before you go in. Do *not*, however, agree to a higher repayment towards your arrears if you cannot afford it. This action won't help anyone in the long term.

When you go into the Hearing, explain what your offer of repayment is and show the District Judge your Personal Budget. If there are very specific reasons why you need to keep the item, explain these to the Judge.

If the Court allows you to keep the item on the basis that you make certain payments, and at a later date you find that you cannot maintain the payments, you should get a form **N244** from the County Court so that you can apply to reduce the payments. Explain on the form why you need to change the payments and attach a new Personal Budget.

Paying County Court Judgments

Forthwith Judgments

If you do not respond to a Court claim or the Court cannot make a decision based on the information that you provide, the Court will make a Forthwith Judgment, which means that the debt has to be paid in full in one payment immediately – this in turn means that the creditor can start enforcement proceedings immediately.

Interest in the County Court

There are two kinds of interest that can be charged in the County Court:

1 Contractual interest – this may be charged for the period from the date of the default to the issue of the County Court claim form.
2 Statutory interest – this may be charged from the date that the Court form is issued to the date that the Court makes the Judgment.

After the Judgment has been made interest can usually only be charged if the debt was not subject to an agreement under the *Consumer Credit Act* 1974 (for information about whether a loan is regulated, see pages 18–20) and the amount of the judgment is £5,000 or more.

Some creditors include a clause in the agreement which says that they can charge contractual interest after Judgment. A recent decision by the Court of Appeal decided that this was an unfair term to include but did not say that the clause had to be removed. It seems likely that a creditor will *not* be able to enforce this clause if instalments have been ordered by the Court. However, the law is still unclear and at the time of writing an appeal to the House of Lords is awaited.

Making payments under a Judgment

You should make your payments to the creditor, not to the Court. If it makes it easier, ask the creditor for payment slips, or, if you have a bank account, you could set up a Standing Order. It is very important that you pay the instalment on time. If payments are late, the creditor could take further action against you (this is called 'enforcement' and is explained on pages 92–101). It is also very important that you pay the instalment exactly as the Judgment says. For example, some people think that if they have to pay a Judgment at £1 per month, then they can send the Court a cheque for £12 which will cover the whole year. Although this may sound sensible, strictly speaking it is not following the exact terms of the payment order and once again the creditor could take enforcement action.

Keep a record of the payments that you make. If you cannot make a payment on time, contact the creditor and explain why. They may agree to let you make the payment on a different date and not take further action against you. Try to get any such agreement in writing or at least the name of the person making a verbal agreement.

If your circumstances change and you cannot afford the repayments, you can apply through the Court to reduce them. You need to complete a form **N245**, which you can collect from the County Court. (A sample of the form is shown on pages 149–150.) There is a £25 fee for making this application, unless you are exempt (see page 103). The **N245** looks like the **N9A** Admission Form (see page 82) and once again you should complete the form with details of your income and expenditure. Contact a money adviser for help if you are uncertain how to complete the form. You should then return it to the Court, keeping a copy. The Court will give the creditor the opportunity to object to your request to change (or 'vary') the instalment. If they do object, Court staff will determine the rate of payment and send both sides a copy of the order. If either side disagrees, they can apply for re-consideration by a District Judge. This will be at your local Court and you should take a copy of your Personal Budget with you. There is no fee for re-consideration.

Enforcement of County Court Judgments

If you do not make the payments that the Court has ordered, or the payments are made late, your creditor can take further action against you (called 'enforcement') to get their money back. In this section we will look at a creditor's options for enforcement and what you can do in response to them. At the time of writing the Government is looking at the various methods of enforcement and some of the procedures may eventually change – the basic principles will remain, however.

Bailiffs

If your creditor wishes to use bailiffs to try and enforce repayment, they will ask the Court to issue a *Warrant of Execution*. This is a notice sent out by the County Court informing you that the County Court bailiffs will be visiting your property, to try and take possessions which can then be sold, unless you make arrangements to pay the debt.

If you receive one of these notices it is important that you do not ignore it but also that you do not panic. Although the notice seems quite intimidating, there are easy ways to deal with it.

Firstly it is important to understand that **bailiffs cannot break into your property and that you are not under any legal obligation to let them in**.

The first time that bailiffs enter your property, they must do so peacefully. This means that they can only enter if you agree to let them in or if a door or window is open or left unlocked (including using ladders to reach upstairs windows). If you have your car parked on your drive, they could take the car without gaining entry to the house. If you know that the bailiffs are coming to your property, you could keep your car in a locked garage or park it elsewhere. If any belongings are kept outside the home, or in a shed or outhouse not attached to the main building, they too can be legally seized.

Once bailiffs have gained peaceful entry into your property, then they can return, and if you refuse to let them in, they can force entry into the property. They must, however, notify you of the date of their return visit. The easiest way to deal with County Court bailiffs is firstly to not let them in and secondly to apply to suspend the *Warrant of Execution* (see below).

If bailiffs *do* enter your home, there are restrictions on the goods which they can take. They cannot take:

- any tools of your trade;
- specific items involved in personal use for employment;
- clothing;

- bedding;
- furniture;
- household equipment;
- provisions for 'basic domestic needs'; or
- goods which do not belong to you – this could include items on Hire Purchase or rental, or things that belong to other people in your home.

If the bailiffs do come to your home, they will not usually take items away on the first occasion. They will usually make a written list of the goods and ask you to sign it. This is called a *Walking Possession Order*. You will normally be expected to make an offer of payment in return for the bailiffs allowing you to continue using the seized goods. Try to stick to a reasonable offer that you can afford. Note that even if you find yourself in this situation you can still apply to suspend the warrant.

Suspending a Warrant of Execution

This is done by making an application on a form **N245** (this is the same form as is used to vary the instalments that the Court has ordered – see page 92 and sample form on pages 149–150 – it can be used to do this and to suspend the warrant at the same time if necessary). You should use your Personal Budget to complete the form. Make sure that you include all your expenditure and repayments towards any other debts. This will help ensure that you make an offer which you can afford and that the Court can see your full circumstances.

You should then send your **N245** to the County Court that issued the Warrant of Execution. There may be a fee to pay (see pages 103–104 on County Court fees). While the Court is considering your application, the bailiffs can still try to visit your home to make a list of your goods but they cannot insist on entering (even though they may say they can).

Once the Court has received your **N245**, it will send a copy to your creditor. If the creditor accepts your offer, they will inform the

Court, which will in turn write to you confirming that the new instalment is acceptable and that the warrant has been suspended.

If the creditor does not agree to your offer, the Court will work out what you should pay based on the information that you have sent them. It is important to note that even though the creditor may not like your offer of repayment the Court may still decide that is what you should pay. If, however, the Court suspends the warrant but on terms you cannot afford, you can apply for re-determination by the District Judge. This procedure is the same as for varying a Judgment (see page 92).

If the creditor objects to the bailiff action being suspended (this may happen if you have consistently missed payments), then there will be a Hearing. You can ask for this to be held at your local County Court. You should attend the Hearing, which will be in the District Judge's office, and take a copy of your Personal Budget.

Charging Orders

Charging Orders enforce a County Court Judgment by making the debt into a secured debt. This means that the debt becomes charged on your property – like a mortgage. Ultimately, a creditor with a Charging Order can apply to the Court to sell your house but this is quite rare and you should seek specialist advice if that happens.

A creditor can only apply for a Charging Order if you have not met the terms of the County Court Judgment. It is very important to remember this, as occasionally a creditor may try to apply for a Charging Order when they are not entitled. There is a 1987 Court of Appeal case called 'Mercantile Credit v Ellis' which you can refer the Court to. If one of your creditors tries to apply for a Charging Order and you are not behind with payments, you should attend the Hearing, taking evidence that you are up to date with your payments and refer to the Mercantile Credit case.

There are two stages in a creditor making an application for a Charging Order:

Stage 1 The creditor makes the application to the County Court. The County Court will check that you have a share (or interest) in the property that the creditor has referred to. If the Court is satisfied that this is the case, it will make what is called a 'Charging Order Nisi'. This does not mean that your creditor has a Charging Order; it just means that the first stage of the process has been completed. The creditor will register the Charge with the Land Registry as an interim measure to prevent you selling the property while the Charging Order process is carried out. A copy of the Charging Order Nisi will then be sent to you, giving you notice of the Hearing (which is the second stage). You will have at least seven days notice of when the Hearing will be.

Stage 2 A Hearing is held in front of a District Judge either at your local County Court or at the Court where the Judgment was obtained. The District Judge will decide whether the Charge on the property should become permanent – this is called a 'Charging Order Absolute'. It is very important that you attend this Hearing: if you do not, the Judge is very likely to make a Charging Order Absolute. If for some reason you cannot attend the Hearing, you should contact the County Court and ask if the Hearing can be rearranged. If you cannot attend because the Court is too far away, write to the Court explaining this and ask for the case to be transferred to your nearest County Court.

How can you prevent a Charging Order Absolute being made?

The District Judge has to decide whether it is reasonable to make a Charging Order and must consider firstly your personal circumstances and secondly whether any of your other creditors would be 'unduly prejudiced' (ie disadvantaged) if a Charging Order was made. What arguments you can use will obviously depend on your circumstances. Some of the possible arguments are listed below:

- If you or a member of your family has a serious illness or disability or are infirm due to old age, then you could argue that a Charging Order would be inappropriate.

- If your property is in joint names with either a partner or member of your family and the debt is in your sole name, you could argue that it would be unfair to the other person to have a Charge put on your property.
- If you have several unsecured creditors, then you could argue that a Charging Order would unfairly favour one specific unsecured creditor over the others. This argument will carry even more weight if you can show the District Judge that you already have payment arrangements in place with your unsecured creditors. All your other unsecured creditors should be informed that the Charging Order Nisi has been made – you could contact them to see if any of them are willing to object to the making of the Charging Order Absolute.
- If your unsecured debts are less than £5,000, you could argue that the debt can be included in an *Administration Order* (see page 104).
- If the debt is quite a small one, particularly when compared to the value of your home, you could argue that it would be unfair to make a Charging Order Absolute.
- If you are involved in divorce proceedings or in a dispute about how a former matrimonial home is to be dealt with, you should get detailed legal advice from the solicitor dealing with this and tell them immediately that a Charging Order Absolute is being considered.

If the Charging Order Absolute is made, it does *not* mean that you will automatically lose your home. You can ask the Court to include in the order that your house is not sold providing you pay the debt in monthly instalments. You should make the offer of instalments at the Hearing, supported by a Personal Budget. If the District Judge will not consider this request at the Hearing, you should make an application afterwards to the Court either on an **N245** or an **N244**, depending on the Court's local practice – check with the Court.

What happens if the creditor applies to the Court for the property to be sold?

Most creditors do not do this – they are often happy to wait for their money until you sell your property. However, if they decide that they do not want to wait, they may apply to the Court for an 'Order For Sale'. If they do this, there will be a Hearing and it will be up to the District Judge to decide if the Order should be made.

Note that the Court will usually only make an Order for Sale if both the debt and the property are in your sole name (or the property and the debt are in the same joint names). If this applies to you, you can still make an offer of payment and ask the Court not to agree to the Order for Sale. It may be that some of the arguments you tried to use to avoid the Charging Order are still applicable, perhaps even more so; if this is the case, you should use them. Particularly the arguments surrounding hardship – if you can prove to the Court that an Order for Sale will mean that someone who is elderly, ill or vulnerable would be made homeless, the District Judge is less likely to make the Order.

Paying off a Charging Order

If you manage to pay off the debt and the costs associated with the Charging Order, you can ask the lender to remove the Charge from your property.

Attachment of Earnings Orders

If you are working, or receive an occupational pension, a creditor can ask the Court that your Judgment be paid directly to them from your wages or pension.

The creditor will make the application to the Court and the Court will send you notice of the application together with a form (called an **N56**). This will ask for details of your income and expenditure and must be returned to the Court within eight days. Your employer must make the payments to your creditor under an Attachment of Earnings Order. The **N56** gives you the opportunity to request a suspended Attachment if you believe that it could affect your employment. This is called a Suspended Attachment of Earnings Order and means that the Attachment is not imposed providing you pay the agreed instalments to the creditor.

You should fill in the details of your income and expenditure on the **N56** form with the information from your Personal Budget. The Court cannot make an Attachment of Earnings Order if your earnings (salary or pension) are below a certain level – this is called the Protected Earnings Rate and is the minimum amount that the Court feels you and your family need to live on. Although Courts do look at your ability to pay when calculating an Attachment of Earnings Order, they use a much stricter system as this is a method of enforcing repayment.

When the Court notifies you of how much will be deducted from your salary or pension, you have 14 days in which to object using the **N244** form. There will then be a Hearing before a District Judge at your local County Court. You should attend the Hearing and take a copy of your Personal Budget and explain why the decided level of deductions from your salary or pension will cause you hardship. If the Attachment will, for example, mean that you cannot afford your housing costs or your Council Tax (both priority payments), you should make this clear to the District Judge.

Consolidated Attachment of Earnings Orders

If you have other County Court Judgments, you can apply for a Consolidated Attachment of Earnings Order. This means that instead of you having to make individual payments to the other creditors who have County Court Judgments, it would be done by your employer and the Court. To apply, you should complete an **N244** including details of the Attachment of Earnings Order already made and your other County Court Judgments.

If you change jobs, or have a period of unemployment and then get a new job, you must inform the Court.

Oral Examinations

An Oral Examination is not strictly a method of enforcement but allows the creditor to ask questions to establish which is the best enforcement method to use. It is something that a creditor can apply for even if you are up to date with your payments. An Oral Examination may involve you attending a Hearing at the County Court, where, on oath, you will be asked questions about your financial circumstances.

Depending on local practice, the Court will either send you a form to complete and return giving information about your financial circumstances, or a notice informing you of the time and date for an Oral Examination. It is an offence not to attend, so if for some reason you cannot attend on the set date (for example because of a hospital appointment), you should write to the Court explaining why and asking for the Court to change the date.

When you attend the Hearing, take a copy of your Personal Budget and any copies of correspondence between you and the creditor. It will also be helpful to take details of your bank account, your mortgage provider and any other evidence suggested in the notice. The Hearing will take normally place in the District Judge's office. The District Judge or Court staff will ask you quite searching questions (usually from a set questionnaire) and will want to know details of any bank accounts that you have. It is important that you answer all the questions truthfully. If there are specific things that you wish to explain, make brief notes before the Hearing so that you remember them. You should not be ordered to do anything at this Hearing, which is to gather information only.

Garnishee Orders

A Garnishee Order allows a creditor to force someone who 'owes' you money or holds your money (ie your bank) to pay it direct to them instead of you. It is an unusual method of enforcement for a creditor to choose because of the difficulty in finding your bank account and identifying when there is money in it.

It is a two-stage process. The creditor has to apply to the County Court for a 'Garnishee Order Nisi'. This is a temporary order which is sent to your bank. Your bank will then have to freeze your account, up to the amount of the County Court Judgment. The

Garnishee only attaches to the amount of money that is in your account on the day that the bank receives the Order. You will be sent notification of the Garnishee Order seven days after the Bank receives its notification.

The next stage will be a Hearing at which you will be given the chance to explain why the Garnishee Order should not be made 'Absolute'. You should attend the Hearing and explain, for example, that taking that amount of money will cause you severe hardship and offer to make a regular monthly payment.

If your account has been frozen and you need the money urgently to pay for essential living expenses, you should apply for an 'Expedited Hearing'. You should write a letter to the Court explaining why a Hearing needs to happen immediately. You may also need to attach an *affidavit* (**N285** – see sample on page 129): ask the Court if this is necessary.

There is every chance that the Court will make an Order Absolute. However, you can try to use one of the following arguments:

- The account is a joint account but the debt is in the name of only one of the account holders. As the law currently stands, a Garnishee Order Absolute cannot be made in these circumstances.
- The debt could be paid off relatively quickly in instalments.
- Severe hardship will be caused to you or members of your family, for example if taking the money would create other more serious debts, such as mortgage arrears.

If you are unsuccessful in preventing the Order from being made Absolute, the bank will be ordered to pay to the creditor either the amount that was frozen or the amount of the debt, whichever is the lesser.

How to set aside a County Court Judgment

If a County Court Judgment has been entered against you and you think it should not have been, it may be possible for you to 'set the

Judgment aside'. This does not necessarily mean that the Court action stops or that you no longer have to pay the debt. It does, however, take the Court action back to the beginning of the process (ie the Claim stage) and gives you the opportunity to formally dispute the debt if you wish to.

The Court *must* set the Judgment aside if:

1 it was made before the time limit for you to reply to the County Court Claim had expired;
2 the Judgment orders that you pay the debt in full (a Default Judgment) even though you applied to pay in instalments; or
3 you paid the whole debt before the Court made the Judgment.

If you wish to apply to set a Judgment aside, you need to complete an **N244**. On the **N244** include details of the creditor and the Claim number, in the box (in the top right-hand corner).

In Part A you should put what you are asking for – ie that the Judgment be set aside – and also the reason why you are making this request.

In Part B you should tick the box which says 'evidence in Part C in support of my application'.

In Part C you should explain briefly why the Judgment should be set aside and why you think that you have a good chance of successfully disputing the debt.

You should then sign the Statement of Truth and hand in the form to your local County Court. You may have to pay a fee (see pages 103–104 on Court fees).

The Court may decide to set the Judgment aside without a Hearing. If, however, there is a Hearing, it will be at your local County Court in front of a District Judge in their offices. You must attend the Hearing and take any evidence to back up your application. Make notes before the Hearing to help remind you of what you need to say.

Credit repair companies

You may see adverts in the newspapers from companies who claim that they can remove County Court Judgments from your *credit reference file* for a fee. If you have genuine grounds for setting aside a Judgment, you do not need to use these companies as the Court process explained above exists for you. Most advice agencies will be able to help you make the application free of charge (although there may be a Court fee), so there is no need to pay anyone to do it for you. If you do not really have genuine grounds for setting aside a Judgment these companies may still encourage you to use their services but this is *not* recommended as you could get into trouble with the County Court.

If you have used a credit repair company in a genuine attempt to get a County Court Judgment removed and they did not do what they promised, you should contact your local Trading Standards office and complain – the phone number will be in the local council listings in the phone book.

County Court fees

This section briefly explains the rules relating to fees payable to the County Court. These fees have to be paid when an application is made.

The most common fees are currently:

- Suspending a *Warrant of Execution* or varying a Judgment (**N245**): £25.
- Setting aside a County Court Judgment (**N244**): £50.
- Applying to vary an *Attachment of Earnings Order* (**N244**): £50.

Details of other fees payable are available from your local County Court.

Some people are exempt from paying Court fees. If you receive either Income Support or income-based Jobseekers Allowance (JSA), you can apply for exemption. You must provide the Court with proof that you receive these benefits – a recent letter from the Benefits Agency or a photocopy of your Order Book will be sufficient.

If you receive either Working Families Tax Credit or Disabled Persons Tax Credit, you will be exempt if you get either the maximum tax credit or if less than £70 per week has been taken off the maximum tax credit payable. You can tell whether this applies to you by looking at the letter that explains your benefit to you. You should then use this letter as proof for the Court.

If you are eligible for exemption from the Court fee, fill in form **EX160** (available from your local County Court) with details of the debt and your creditor and also your name and address. You should then tick the box that shows which benefit you get. You can ignore the rest of the form but be sure to sign it on the back.

If you do not receive any of these benefits but will nevertheless struggle to pay the fee, you can apply for the fee to be reduced or waived. The Court may choose to reduce the fee but still expect you to pay some of it. You will need to fill in the **EX160** (Application for a Fee Exemption or Remission) as above. You should then hand this into the County Court with your main application. The Court will notify you of its decision. Note, however, that it is very difficult to get County Court fees reduced, even where it is clear that payment of the fee will cause hardship.

Administration Orders

These are Court orders that deal with all your unsecured credit debts (ie not secured on your house), such as credit card debts and some priority debts. In effect the debts are all 'put into one basket'. You then make one payment into the Court and the Court is responsible for sending the payments to your creditors.

To be able to apply for an Administration Order you must have:

- a Court Judgment (either County or High Court);
- have at least two debts; and
- your total debts must not exceed £5,000.

Administration Orders are advantageous for a number of reasons:

- If you have a lot of creditors it takes away the burden (and cost) of having to send off several cheques or postal orders every month.
- All the creditors listed in your application for an Administration Order are prohibited from taking any other action against you unless they get the Court's permission first. This applies even if they are subsequently not included in the Order.
- Unlike many of the other applications that you have to make in the County Court, there is no upfront fee to pay. The fee is added to the total debt on the Administration Order, currently at a rate of 10 per cent of the amount paid.
- If you have an Administration Order you can apply for something called a *Composition Order* (see pages 108–110). This can enable you to limit how long you have to make payments into the Administration Order.

To apply for an Administration Order you need to complete a form called an **N92** – you can get this from your local County Court. (A sample form is shown on pages 145–148.) The form may not seem complicated to fill in but various problems can arise because different courts adopt slightly different approaches to the information that you provide. You may want to seek advice from a local money advice agency as it may have an idea of how your local County Court treats certain items.

Filling in your Administration Order application

On the first page in the top right-hand corner you need to put in the name of a County Court. This should be your local County Court, which may not be the Court from where your County Court Judgment was issued. If you are in doubt as to the name of your local County Court, contact a local advice agency.

On the first page space is provided for you to put details of all your debts. You should include all the creditors' addresses, reference numbers and amounts that you owe. If the debt is with a Collection

Agency (which collects on behalf of the company you owe money to), you should put the name of the original creditor and then put 'care of' and then the name and address of the Collection Agency. If you have borrowed any money in joint names with someone else, you should still put down the full amount of the debt and details of the other person who is jointly liable with you. Once you have listed all your debts, you should put the total at the bottom of this space.

The rest of the form asks for personal details – your employment details and family circumstances. There is then a section for details of your income and expenditure; you should use the information from your Personal Budget (see pages 27–29).

You also need to put details of any arrears on priority debts that you have and the amount that you pay towards them in this section. If you have any arrears payments deducted from any State Benefits that you receive, you should make this clear. Make sure that you only use monthly or weekly figures – do not mix the two (see page 29 for how to work this out). You may like to use monthly figures as on the back page of the form there is a box which asks you to put how much you can afford per month towards the Administration Order. This should be based on what you have available after you have met all your essential expenditure. If you are on Income Support (Minimum Income Guarantee) or other State Benefits, a reasonable figure might be £4 per month, but could be as little as £1 a month.

Do *not* sign the bottom of the form until you are at the County Court and with the member of staff who is looking at your application. This section is a declaration that the information on the form is correct and you *must* sign it in front of a Court Officer.

When you hand in the form, you will need to show the Court staff a copy of your County Court Judgment. If you cannot find the original, you should contact the Court where action was taken against you – they may be able to provide you with a copy of the Judgment.

Once your application has been handed in, the County Court will either make the Order without a Hearing and write to all your creditors giving them 16 days in which to object, or it will order a Hearing – which you must attend.

Some creditors may object because they think that your offer of repayment is too low. Others may object to being included in the Order because they can collect the debt some other way. Creditors who may commonly object are those collecting Council Tax, gas and electricity debts.

If none of your creditors object and your application is accepted by the Court, then the Order will be made and you will be notified in writing.

If any of your creditors do object, there will be a Hearing. You will be notified of the date of the Hearing. It is very important that you attend so that you can argue against any objections made by your creditors. Your arguments will depend on which creditor has objected and why. If any creditors do object, you may wish to seek specialist advice from one of the agencies listed in Chapter 1.

Once your Administration Order is made, then providing you make the payments, no further action can be taken by any of your creditors. If you miss payments the Court may 'revoke' (cancel) your Administration Order. If your circumstances change and you can no longer afford to meet the original repayment, you should apply either by letter or on an **N244** form to reduce the payment. There should not be any fee for this.

If any of the creditors who you listed in your original application for an Administration Order try to take any enforcement action against you and you have not missed any payments, you should write to them pointing out that an Administration Order is in place and that they cannot take further action without the Court's permission. If they persist, you should contact the County Court.

An Administration Order will last until you have cleared the debts in full unless you apply for a *Composition Order* (see below). During this time you will be expected *not* to take on any additional debts.

After his wife died, **Mr Hussain** was quite depressed and for some months did not really take much notice of his bills or bank statements. Eventually he gathered his bills together and he and his son looked through them. He had missed several payments on a catalogue bill and as there had been no correspondence with the company, they had obtained a County Court Judgment against Mr Hussain. This was now due for payment. His credit card company had issued a Default Notice. There were also several small debts outstanding with home credit companies and Mr Hussain was also overdrawn at the bank by £450. When he looked at his income and expenditure it was clear that he was not going to be able to pay all these debts immediately. He did, however, remember seeing some information about Administration Orders. He contacted a local advice agency and discovered that he could apply for one of these as he had a County Court Judgment and his debts totalled £3,800 (less than £5,000). He applied for an Administration Order, which was granted without a Hearing. As a result he was able to make one payment per month into the County Court and not worry about having to remember all his payments every month.

Composition Orders

If a Composition Order is granted, it means that you do not have to pay your debts in full; you will only have to pay a proportion of them, usually for three years. You can apply for a Composition Order to be made on your Administration Order either when you initially make your Administration Order application or after a period of time. Some District Judges do not like to grant Composition Orders straightaway – they may want to see proof of your commitment to paying the Order for six months for example.

If you apply for a Composition Order when you initially apply for your Administration Order, you should make this request in the box on the back page of the application where it says '*Is there anything else you would like the Court to take into consideration?*'

If you apply for a Composition at a later date, you should use an **N244** application form. There is no fee for this.

Working out your Composition Order

You have to work Composition Orders out yourself:

1 Work out what you owe in total.
2 Work out how much you want to pay back per month on your Administration Order (from your Personal Budget).
3 Work out how long you want to pay the Order for – the usual time is three years. For this calculation you should use the number of months (so three years would be 36 months).
4 Multiply your offer of payment by the number of instalments you want to pay.
5 Divide that figure by your total debt.
6 Multiply by 100.
7 This will give you the % in the pound and pence per pound of your debt that you will pay back.

Mr Khan owes £3,600 which he can afford to repay at £20 per month. He wishes to repay this over three years (36 months).

£20 per month × 36 months = £720

720 ÷ 3,600 = 1/5

1/5 x 100 = 20 (pence in the pound or 20%).

> If this Composition Order was granted, then Mr Khan would pay
> £20 per month for three years and at the end of that time the
> Order would finish and the remaining debts would be written off.
> This would be described as paying 'to the extent of 20p in the £'.

Common Problems with Administration Orders

Priority debts – the guidance on Administration Orders tells you that you have to include details of all your debts; this would include rent or mortgage arrears. Because these types of debt can be very large, their inclusion may well take you over the £5,000 limit. It is very likely that these kinds of creditors would object to being included on the Administration Order anyway. If you have to include these types of debt, put them at the end of the list of creditors, keeping them separate from the total of your unsecured credit debt. Put a note on the form explaining that these are priority debts and that you have a separate arrangement. If the priority creditor has already taken Court action (for example your mortgage lender already has a Suspended Possession Order), make this clear.

No available income – often when people are on a low income and complete a Personal Budget, there is no available money to pay their unsecured creditors. Some Court staff or District Judges may refuse to grant you an Administration Order if this is the case. If this applies to you, then in the section *'is there anything else you want the Court to know'* you should explain that although you have no available income you think that you could budget to ensure that you make a payment every month. If there is a Hearing before a District Judge, you could explain to the Judge that you have been maintaining payments on the County Court Judgment already. If the Court refuses your Order without explanation, write to the Court Manager to seek an explanation. Once you receive this, contact a local advice agency for further advice on the response.

Council Tax/Community Charge arrears – often councils will object to having these arrears included on the Administration Order as they should be treated as a priority debt. There is a case called *Preston Borough Council v Riley (1995)* which you can use to argue that these arrears should be included on your Administration Order. If you need a copy or summary of this case, contact a local advice agency.

Magistrates Court fines/Social Fund loans – these debts are often left out of Administration Orders by District Judges as some Courts do not consider them to be ordinary debts. Until your application has been considered you should keep paying the Magistrates Court fine. If the Social Fund loan is included, the Benefits Agency may still continue to deduct payments from your benefits. If this is the case, contact the County Court.

If you are considering applying for an Administration Order, you may want to seek advice from one of the agencies listed in Chapter 1.

Time Orders

The County Court can grant a Time Order which can change certain aspects of a loan. The Order may change:

- the interest rate;
- how much has to be paid every month; or
- how long the loan will last.

Time Orders are usually used to deal with loans secured on your property (although they can also be used in relation to a Hire Purchase agreement). A Time Order can be a useful tool if you have a secured loan and the lender is trying to repossess your home or is charging a very high interest rate.

You can only apply for a Time Order if the loan you have is regulated by the *Consumer Credit Act* 1974. Normally loans taken out before 1 May 1998, and for £15,000 or less, are regulated by this Act. Since 1 May 1998 this limit has increased to £25,000. Loans that you take out to buy your home from a bank or building society are *not* covered by the Consumer Credit Act. Your loan agreement should make it clear whether or not the loan is regulated by the Act. If you are unsure, contact a local advice agency or Trading Standards Office to check.

You can only apply for a Time Order at certain times. Usually this will be:

- when a creditor has issued a *Default Notice*; or
- when they have already started or taken Court action.

If you apply when the creditor has issued a Default Notice, you will need to make the application on an **N440**. This currently costs £120 (but see pages 103–104 on exemptions).

If the creditor has already issued Court proceedings, you should request a Time Order on the Reply Form. If the Possession Hearing has already taken place and the creditor has a Possession Order, you should make the application on an **N244**. The fee for this is currently £50 (but see pages 103–104).

A Time Order can deal either with the arrears on a loan or with the whole amount outstanding under the loan. Which you can apply for will depend on the details in the *Default Notice*. If the Default Notice *only* relates to the arrears, then the Time Order can only deal with the arrears – for example you may ask for the interest that is being charged on the arrears to be reduced but you will still have to pay the contractual instalment. In most cases a Default Notice 'calls in' (deals with) the whole amount outstanding under the loan. If this is the case, the Time Order can deal with the whole loan.

A Court of Appeal case in 1995 clarified the powers of the Court in relation to Time Orders. The Court said that the whole amount of money owed could be included in the Time Order and that, if the Court felt it was 'just to do so', then the instalments and the interest rates could be altered. The case is called *Southern and District Finance plc v Barnes*. If you want to see more details of this case, contact a local advice agency.

Key points

- Never ignore Court papers and always respond to a County Court document within the time limit.

- Always attend Hearings.

- Always be realistic in the offers you make at Court.

- Seek advice if you are uncertain about anything.

- If you hear from bailiffs, don't panic. You have rights. Get advice if you need help in completing the forms.

- Other ways of enforcing a debt include: a Charging Order against your property, 'attaching' your earnings or pension; and Garnishee Orders freezing your bank account.

- If you have several debts, totalling not more than £5,000, you may want to apply for an Administration Order in which the County Court will manage your repayments for you.

- You may also want to look into a Composition Order which would allow the Court to reduce the total amount of debt owed.

- You could also check whether you are entitled to apply for a Time Order under the Consumer Credit Act.

7 Bankruptcy

This chapter covers:

- *The advantages and disadvantages of bankruptcy*
- *The procedure for making yourself bankrupt*
- *The effects of bankruptcy*
- *How to argue against a creditor making you bankrupt*
- *Cancelling bankruptcy orders*
- *Alternatives to bankruptcy*

Bankruptcy can be a way of dealing with debt problems and it can also be a way that creditors try to enforce repayment. You can choose to make yourself bankrupt, or a creditor can make you bankrupt (providing you owe more than £750 to an individual creditor). Although the procedures for these two methods are different, the effects are the same. This chapter looks at both methods; it deals with making yourself bankrupt first.

The advantages and disadvantages of bankruptcy

Making yourself bankrupt is a serious step as the effects of bankruptcy can be far-reaching. You should consider the advantages and disadvantages very carefully; they will depend very much on your own personal circumstances.

Advantages

- If you know that you will have to pay your debts over a very long period of time and you do not want that to be the case, bankruptcy can provide 'light at the end of the tunnel'. In bankruptcy your debts are written off after two or three years, depending on your total level of debt. After that you can make a fresh start, free of debt.
- While you are bankrupt (known as 'undischarged'), your creditors cannot contact you directly or take any further action against you.
- It can relieve the intolerable pressures of being in debt.

Disadvantages

- If you have any assets, these may be taken from you and sold to raise money to pay your debts (this will be looked at in more detail on pages 121–122).
- You may lose your home.
- The law places various restrictions on undischarged bankrupts.
- Whilst you are bankrupt, you will be unable to take out credit of over £250 without disclosing that you are an undischarged bankrupt. Even after discharge you may find it hard to get credit.
- There may be other adverse effects depending on your personal circumstances (see pages 119–121).

The procedure for making yourself bankrupt

Completing the paperwork

To make yourself bankrupt you need to complete a Debtor's Petition and Statement of Affairs – you can get these from your local Bankruptcy Court (usually the County Court or High Court in London, but check first). If both you and your spouse or partner are going bankrupt, you will each need to complete separate forms. An example of the paperwork is provided in the Appendices on pages 130–142.

The Petition is fairly simple to fill in and you can delete any of the form that does not apply to you. If you are not sure, ask for help from an advice agency or from the Court staff.

The Statement of Affairs has an *affidavit* on the first page – you should *not* sign this until you are actually ready to go bankrupt and are presenting the forms to the Court Officer.

On the second page you need to put details of any secured creditors that you have, which may include your mortgage.

On the third page there is space for you to list all your unsecured creditors, including Hire Purchase. These should be listed in alphabetical order and you should fill in their addresses and account numbers. You must include details of *all* your debts. In the 'amount owed' box you can put the amount to the nearest pound: you do not have to put down the pence.

If you have a debt in joint names with someone else and they are not going bankrupt, the creditor will still be able to pursue them for the debt even though the debt will be included in your bankruptcy.

The next section (see page 136) asks for details of your assets – this includes details of any bank accounts and other savings. Even if you have accounts with only a few pounds in them, you should include their details. You should then list any other assets that you own. Even though you have to list your assets, the *Official Receiver* may decide that some of them are not worth selling, because they are of little value for example, and you may be able to keep them. This applies to most household items unless they are of high value.

You have to provide details of any dependants (people who live with you and are reliant on you) and also whether any of your creditors have used bailiffs or the County Court to enforce debts.

The next section (see page 139) asks for details of any arrangements that you have tried to come to with your creditors. If you have previously tried to negotiate reduced repayments with your creditors, you should include the details in this section.

The final section (shown on page 141) is a Statement of Means where you need to list all your income and expenditure. If you have done a Personal Budget, you can transfer the information from that. Make sure you include *all* your essential expenditure.

You should sign and date the bottom of each page of the Statement of Affairs when you take it to Court.

Taking the Petition to the Court

Once you have completed your Petition, you will need to take it and two further copies to your local County Court. There is a fee for making yourself bankrupt. The first part of the fee is a deposit of

£250 which has to be paid by everybody, regardless of their means, and is a contribution to the Official Receiver's fee for the initial administration of your bankruptcy. The second part of the fee is £120 which is the Court fee – you may be exempt from paying this part of the fee or you may be able to apply for the fee to be reduced (see page 104). If both you and your partner are going bankrupt, you will each have to pay the fee.

If you need to save for several months to be able to afford the bankruptcy fee, you can write to all your creditors explaining this and asking them not to take any action in the meantime.

At the Court, the staff will give you a receipt for your fee and take your forms. You will then have to wait to see a District Judge, although in some Courts an appointment may be made for another day. The District Judge will check the paperwork and if everything is satisfactory you will normally be declared bankrupt. If your debts are less than £20,000, you can ask the Court to issue a Certificate for Summary Administration. You are still bankrupt but the procedure used to deal with your case will be slightly different and you will only be bankrupt for two years, instead of three. If this applies to you, ask the Court for 'Summary Administration'. It may have a form you can fill in, but this depends on local practice.

The Official Receiver

After you have been certified bankrupt, the Court staff will contact the Official Receiver to arrange an appointment at their office. If your Court does not do this, then the Official Receiver's staff will contact you to arrange an appointment.

The Official Receiver is an official who is responsible for dealing with your bankruptcy and also ensuring that you do not dispose of any assets that you may have. The Official Receiver will investigate your financial affairs before and during your bankruptcy to check that you have not tried to hide any assets and that you have not conducted your financial affairs improperly.

The Official Receiver has to report to your creditors and may also need to report to the Court. The Official Receiver will inform your local authority and the utility companies that you are bankrupt. It also has the power to contact banks, mortgage lenders, insurance companies and other organisations or people who it is thought may have details of any of your assets or debts.

The Official Receiver becomes the 'Trustee' of your estate. This means that it is responsible for disposing of any assets you have and for paying your creditors. Sometimes the Official Receiver will select an Insolvency Practitioner to be your Trustee – Insolvency Practitioners are licensed individuals who specialise in insolvency work.

Before your appointment you will be asked to complete a form with details of all your assets and debts. Complete the form as thoroughly as you can. If there is anything that you do not understand, make a note of it so that you can ask at your appointment. The Official Receiver may want to see recent bank statements and recent creditor correspondence. If you have previously run a business, it will want to see the last set of business accounts.

At your appointment you will be interviewed by an 'examiner', who is a member of the Official Receiver's staff. They will ask for details of any assets you have and also want you to explain what led to your bankruptcy. This procedure is formal and may sound a little intimidating, but it is straightforward. Give the examiner all the facts and tell the truth. In some areas, interviews with the Official Receiver's Office are conducted over the telephone; the questions asked will still be the same.

What happens next will largely depend on how complicated your case is and whether or not you have any assets. If you have provided all the details that the Official Receiver requires and you have no assets and no available income, it is unlikely that you will hear from the Official Receiver's Office again. However, if your circumstances change (for example if you come into money or your income increases), then you must inform the Official Receiver's Office immediately.

If you have any assets, the Official Receiver will call a creditors meeting so that someone (usually an Insolvency Practitioner) can be appointed as Trustee.

If you have a certain level of available income after your essential expenditure has been met, the Official Receiver may make an Income Payments Order. This means that you will have to make a monthly payment towards your debts.

It is very important that you co-operate with the Official Receiver. If you do not, it can apply to the County Court for your public examination. This means that you will be questioned, on oath, in open court, about your finances. It also means that your bankruptcy may be extended beyond the normal two or three years.

The effects of bankruptcy

If you are made bankrupt, some of the outcomes are:

- You must not try to obtain credit of more than £250 without telling the creditor that you are an undischarged bankrupt.
- You cannot run a business in a different name (from that in which you went bankrupt) without telling anyone with whom you do business the name in which you went bankrupt.
- Initially your bank account is frozen when you are made bankrupt. Even when the Official Receiver releases the account, you may find that your bank or building society will close your account. If this is the case, and you need a bank account for wages or a pension to be paid into, you should be able to open a basic account with one of the high street banks. This account will give you access to a cash machine but will not allow you to go overdrawn or have cheque book facilities.
- Your utility and phone suppliers may be reluctant to provide you with a service based on credit, although fuel suppliers cannot refuse a supply simply because you are bankrupt. The companies may ask you to pay a deposit, provide a guarantee or have a prepayment meter fitted (see page 47). If you share your home with someone, the companies may want the bills put into their name.

- If you are still working, some jobs are affected by bankruptcy; accountancy is one example. Check your terms and conditions or speak to someone in your union or welfare office. In some cases being bankrupt can lead to dismissal.
- You cannot run a limited company or become a company director without the Court's permission.
- You cannot hold public office (eg be a local councillor or Justice of the Peace) or be a trustee of a charity.
- You should not make payments to any of your unsecured creditors any more. However, you should keep paying essential items such as your mortgage, ongoing Council Tax and any Magistrates Court fines that you have. If any of your unsecured creditors continue to contact you, inform the Official Receiver's Office *immediately*.
- If you own an item on Hire Purchase (HP), the HP company will be informed of your bankruptcy. Most HP companies will then terminate your agreement and ask for the goods to be returned. You may be able to negotiate with the company to keep the goods if you can afford the payment and your Trustee agrees.
- If you rent your home, bankruptcy will not normally affect this. However, you should check the terms of your tenancy agreement. Note that even though rent arrears are written off in bankruptcy, the landlord may still be able to evict you for non-payment.
- You may have to make payments under an Income Payments Order. This should only happen if your income is higher than average and you have a large amount of available income (for example more than £100 per month) after you have met all your essential expenditure. This Order would normally only last for as long as your bankruptcy.
- Once you are bankrupt, that fact will be advertised in the *London Gazette*, which is a publication that carries legal notices. It will also be advertised in your local paper, although only in the small notices section.
- If the Official Receiver finds that you have committed any offences prior to the bankruptcy, you could be fined or imprisoned, although this is extremely rare. Examples of behaviour which could lead to fines or imprisonment include trying to avoid

paying creditors by giving assets away, not keeping proper accounts if you have been running a business, or running up debt by gambling.

■ If you own any assets of value, these could be sold by your Trustee.

Assets

Household goods

Basic household goods are not usually of interest to the Trustee – this includes items such as bedding, furniture, and basic household equipment. The value of items such as televisions or stereos will determine whether or not you can keep them. If they are expensive and up-to-date models then they may be sold. Other items such as antiques may also be sold. If you have a car it may be sold, depending on its value and whether it is essential.

Your home

If you own your own house, then the Trustee could force the sale of the property. This will depend on the value of the property, the equity (ie the difference between the value of the property and any secured debt outstanding) and whether you own it solely or with someone else. If you have a husband/wife or dependent children living with you who have not gone bankrupt, it may be possible for the sale of the property to be put off for 12 months, giving you time to find somewhere else to live.

If you own the property jointly, then the Trustee would only be entitled to your share of the equity in the house. If it is possible, someone – your partner, or a friend or relative – may be able to buy out your share of the property from the Trustee. If there is little equity in the property or negative equity, the offer may not need to be high. If you think that you know someone who may be willing to do this, they should seek legal advice as soon as possible.

If there is little or no equity and no one offers to buy out your interest, the Trustee will not wish to sell the property straightaway. Instead, the Trustee will place a Charge on the property which will be to the value of the total sum owed plus the Trustee's own fees. This amount would then be paid off from your share of any profits that result from the eventual sale of the property at some time in the future.

It is very important that you try to find someone to buy out your interest while you are still bankrupt. Otherwise your Trustee can come back and sell your property at any time after your bankruptcy has ended.

Your pension

Since 2000, any pension which has been approved by the Inland Revenue, will be protected from being taken by your Trustee. Your State Pension is also protected. It is only if your total household income exceeds what the Trustee regards as reasonable domestic needs that you will be asked to pay anything towards your debts.

If you are still making payments into a personal pension when you go bankrupt, it may not be worthwhile continuing to make the payments. You should seek advice from an independent financial adviser about this.

Mr and Mrs Gordon had run a private day care centre for disabled people. Unfortunately, their business failed and they found themselves with serious debts as a result. Their home was repossessed due to a second mortgage on the property, and after the house was sold there was still a debt of £35,000. In addition they owed the Inland Revenue £4,000, suppliers £3,400 and their bank £12,000. They were rehoused into a rented property by the council but because they were both in their 60s they found it difficult to find any new employment and were very worried that they would never be able to pay off their debts as they were relying on the Basic State Pension.

They approached a local advice agency which suggested to them that they might consider going bankrupt as they had a high level of debts with no likelihood of repaying them. Mr and Mrs Gordon were worried at the prospect of going bankrupt but once it was made clear that they had little to lose – as they had no assets which would have to be sold – they felt a little more confident. As the debts were in joint names, they both needed to go bankrupt and so they each had to pay the bankruptcy fee, which their daughter agreed to give them.

They completed the bankruptcy petitions and then took them to the County Court. After they had paid their fee they briefly went before a District Judge. It was then arranged for them to be interviewed by a member of the Official Receiver's Office. They were very apprehensive about this but it was not the ordeal they had feared as they were able to provide the Receiver's Office with all the information required. As their income was so low, Mr and Mrs Gordon didn't have to pay anything towards their debts. They felt relieved that their creditors could no longer be constantly contacting them and that at the end of the bankruptcy period they would be free from their debt problems.

How to argue against a creditor making you bankrupt

Any of your unsecured creditors can make you bankrupt if you owe them more than £750. Many unsecured creditors do not use bankruptcy; it tends to be favoured by traders who are owed money through business failure, or by the Inland Revenue, Customs and Excise or credit companies where a debt is owed on a charge card. Often creditors will threaten bankruptcy without intending to follow it through. If a creditor threatens you with bankruptcy, you may wish to contact an advice agency to see if they know whether this is a course of action that the particular creditor frequently adopts.

In some cases when a creditor does begin bankruptcy proceedings, you may not wish to dispute them. You may have wanted to go bankrupt but been unable to afford the fee.

If a creditor wishes to make you bankrupt, they must normally (but not always) issue a Statutory Demand. This is a form that will include details of the debt that you owe the creditor. You should not ignore this form unless you want to go bankrupt.

If you don't want to go bankrupt, you have 18 days from receipt of the form in which to apply for the Demand to be 'set aside'. If the Court thinks that you have a case, it will arrange a date for a Hearing. Getting a Statutory Demand set aside can only be done under certain circumstances. Seek specialist advice from one of the agencies listed in Chapter 1 if you don't want to go bankrupt.

You could also try to negotiate informally with the creditor. If you have no assets, you could argue that there is little point in the creditor making you bankrupt as they will not gain financially from it. If being made bankrupt could make you lose your job, you could argue that you will be able to repay the creditor more if your circumstances remain the same and you are not made bankrupt.

If you desperately wish to avoid bankruptcy and you own your own home, you could offer the creditor a *Voluntary Charge* on your property (see page 77). This would mean that you agree to the debt becoming secured on your home – with an offer of instalments. Try to get the creditor to agree that they will not enforce the Charge if payments are made. If you missed an instalment, the creditor could repossess your home. This is a drastic way of trying to avoid bankruptcy and one that you should consider very carefully. It would certainly be worth contacting a local advice agency to discuss the implications of this in your particular circumstances.

If the County Court dismisses your application for set aside, or you do not apply, the creditor can proceed to issue a Bankruptcy Petition. The Court will send a copy to you with a Hearing date and time.

If you wish to oppose the Petition you must do so within seven days of the Hearing. You should use Form **6.19** (obtainable through an advice agency or The Stationery Office) and hand it in at the Court, sending a copy to the creditor and keeping a copy for yourself.

At the Hearing the Court will normally make a Bankruptcy Order if it is clear that you have no reasonable prospect of paying off the debt. If you have made a reasonable offer of repayment but the creditor has turned it down, then you could try to argue that the creditor has unreasonably refused the offer. There are also other legal grounds for opposing a Petition and you may wish to seek advice about these.

Cancelling bankruptcy orders

Discharge

This is when your bankruptcy comes to an end. If you have followed the rules regarding bankruptcy and done everything reasonably required of you by the Trustee, discharge from bankruptcy is automatic either after two years (if your debts were less than £20,000 and you applied for Summary Administration) or three years. You will not normally be informed of this. If you require proof of discharge, you should write to the Court that dealt with your bankruptcy to request a Certificate of Discharge.

If during your bankruptcy you have not co-operated with the Trustee, they may ask the Court to delay your discharge.

Once you have been discharged, most of your debts will be written off at the end of the bankruptcy. There are some debts, however, which you will still have to pay. For example:

- fines;
- debts arising through fraud;
- non-provable debts such as Child Support and maintenance arrears; and
- other orders arising from family proceedings.

Remember that even after discharge, the Official Receiver or Trustee may still have control over your assets – in particular your home.

Annulment

If you believe that there is a legal reason why you should not have been made bankrupt, you can apply for the bankruptcy to be 'annulled'. You may wish to do this for example because the correct procedures were not followed when you were made bankrupt or because all your debts and the Trustee's fees have been paid.

If you want to apply for annulment for any reason other than full payment, you should seek specialist advice. Otherwise the application form can be obtained from the Bankruptcy Court and that Court can advise you on the procedures.

Alternatives to bankruptcy

An Individual Voluntary Arrangement (IVA) is a formal way of making an arrangement with your creditors and avoiding bankruptcy. To be able to apply for an IVA you have to be able to either raise a lump sum and/or make a significant regular payment.

An IVA usually lasts for up to five years and usually involves only paying a proportion of your debts. Negotiation is conducted by an Insolvency Practitioner and the 'Proposals' for repayment are voted on by your creditors. For the IVA to be successful, 75 per cent of the creditors by value (ie creditors whose amounts owed make up 75 per cent of the total debt), who bother to vote, have to agree to the Proposals.

Your local County Court should have a list of Insolvency Practitioners. They charge quite high fees for working on IVAs. Some charge a large fee up front, while others only charge a fee if the IVA is successfully set up and then take their fee from your payments. In some cases if your IVA fails – for example because you do not maintain the arranged payments – you may be made bankrupt.

Another alternative is to come to informal arrangements with your creditors using pro rata offers of repayments. The advantage of an IVA, however, is that it is capable of binding all unsecured creditors, even those who do not accept your offer.

▼

Mrs Stanley was a widow who worked in a bank. She enjoyed the job and had only five years to go until she retired. Unfortunately, the death of her husband several years ago had made it very difficult for her to carry on paying all her debts. Most of the credit that the couple had taken out had been in Mrs Stanley's name so she was still liable to pay it. Also, Mr Stanley had not kept up with his insurance policies and so Mrs Stanley had not received much money after her husband's death. She had reached a point where she could no longer juggle her income and when she added up all her debts found that she owed in excess of £20,000. Several of her creditors were starting to threaten to take further action and Mrs Stanley was very concerned as she was worried that this could affect her job at the bank. Although she could make some payments to her creditors, they would not be at the level that they required.

It was suggested by a friend that she ring an Insolvency Practitioner who could advise on whether an Individual Voluntary Arrangement would be appropriate. This would avoid Court action and also clear her debts within five years. The Insolvency Practitioner took details of her debts, available income and assets (which were £3,000 in savings). The Insolvency Practitioner then contacted her to say that he felt that her creditors would agree to an IVA if she paid her £3,000 in to the IVA and paid £300 each month. As Mrs Stanley had chosen an Insolvency Practitioner who took his fee at a small amount each month rather than one large up-front fee, she felt that this was an option that she could afford. A sufficient number of the creditors agreed to the proposals and Mrs Stanley was able to repay her debts over roughly five years.

Key points

- Think carefully and get proper advice before opting for bankruptcy.

- You need to complete a Bankruptcy Petition and Statement of Affairs.

- Don't sign the affidavit until you are with a Court official.

- You have to pay a fee of at least £250 to the Court.

- The Official Receiver will inform all your creditors of your bankruptcy.

- The Receiver becomes Trustee of your assets. You must co-operate with them.

- Your bank account will be frozen but may be released later.

- You will be able to keep your essential household equipment and furniture.

- If you are a homeowner, and there is equity in your house, it is likely to be sold.

- An Individual Voluntary Arrangement (IVA) is an alternative to bankruptcy.

Appendices – sample forms

1 General Form of an Affidavit (N285)

General form of affidavit

Claimant

Defendant

(1) Full names and occupation of deponent.

(2) Address

(3) Set out in numbered paragraphs, the facts deposed to.

I (1)

of (2)

make oath and say as follows:- (3)

Sworn by	on
(deponent)	
This is the	affidavit
(1st, 2nd, etc.)	
filed on behalf of	by this deponent
(party)	
on	
(date filed)	

In the

Court

Claim No.

Sworn at   in the

County of

this   day of   [19][20]

Before me

Officer of a Court, appointed by the Judge to take Affidavits.

N285 - w3 General form of affidavit (4.99)

Printed on behalf of The Court Service

2 Debtor's Bankruptcy Petition Form 6.27

Rule 6.37   **Form 6.27**

Debtor's Bankruptcy Petition
(TITLE)

(a) Insert full name, address and occupation (if any) of debtor

I a)_____

_____

_____   _____]

(b) Insert in full any other name(s) by which the debtor is or has been known
(c) Insert former address or addresses at which the debtor may have incurred debts or liabilities still unpaid or unsatisfied

also known as (b)_____

[lately residing at (c)_____]

[and carrying on business as (d)_____

_____

_____   _____

_____

_____]

(d) Insert trading name (adding "with another or others", if this is so), business address and nature of the business.

[and lately carrying on business as (e)_____

_____

_____

_____

_____   _____]

(e) Insert any former trading names (adding "with another or others", if this is so), business address and nature of the business in respect of which the debtor may have incurred debts or liabilities still unpaid or unsatisfied
(f) Delete as applicable

request the court that a bankruptcy order be made against me and say as follows:-

1. I have for the greater part of six months immediately preceding the presentation of this petition (f) [resided at] [carried on business at]_____   _____

_____

within the district of (f) [this court] (j)_____county court. I am presenting my petition to this court, as it is the nearest full-time county court to (j)_____ county court, for the following reasons:

(g) State reasons   (g)

2. I am unable to pay my debts.
3. (f) That within the period of five years ending with the date on

this petition:-

    (i)   I have not been adjudged bankrupt

OR

(h) Insert date   I was adjudged bankrupt on (h)   in the (j)

(j) Insert name of court

(k) Insert number of bankruptcy proceedings   Court No. (k)

    (ii)   I have not (f) [made a composition with my creditors in satisfaction of my (S.16 debts] or (f) [entered into a scheme of arrangement with creditors] BA 1914)

OR

On (h)_____I (f) [made a composition] [entered into a scheme of arrangement] with my creditors.

    (iii)   I have not entered into a voluntary arrangement

OR

On (h)_____I entered into a voluntary arrangement

    (iv)   I have not been subject to an administration order under Part VI of the County Courts Act 1984

OR

On (h)_____ an administration order was made

against me in the (j)_____county court.

4. A statement of my affairs is filed with this petition.

Date_____

Signature_____

Complete only if petition not heard immediately

Endorsement

This petition having been presented to the court on_____
_____it is ordered that the petition shall be heard as follows:-

Date_____

Time_____hours

Place_____

---

3 Statement of Affairs (Debtor's Petition) Form 6.28

Form 6.28
(Rule 6.L1)

Statement of Affairs (Debtor's Petition)
Insolvency Act 1986

NOTE:
These details will
be the same as
those shown at the
top of your
petition

In the _____

In Bankruptcy

NO_____ of 200_____

Re _____

The 'Guidance Notes' Booklet tells you how to complete this form easily and correctly

Show your current financial position by completing all the pages of this form which will then be your Statement of Affairs

---

AFFIDAVIT

This Affidavit must be sworn by a Solicitor or Commissioner of Oaths or an officer of the court duly authorised to administer oaths when you have completed the rest of this form

(a) Insert full name and occupation

1 (a)_____

_____

(b) Insert full address

of (b)_____

_____

_____

Make oath and say that the several pages marked

_____

and contained in the exhibit marked "Z"

are to the best of my knowledge and belief a full, true and complete statement of my affairs at today's date.

Sworn at _____

Dated this_____day of_____200__ Signature(s)_____
Before me_____

A Solicitor or Commissioner of Oaths or Duly authorised officer

Before swearing the affidavit, the Solicitor or Commissioner is particularly requested to make sure that the full name, address and description of the deponent are stated, and to initial any crossing-out or other alterations in the printed form. A deficiency in the affidavit in any of the above respects will mean it will be refused by the court, and will need to be re-sworn.

3a List of Secured Creditors

LIST OF SECURED CREDITORS

^A

Is anyone claiming something of yours to clear or reduce their claim?

If **'YES'** give details below:

Tick Box
YES   NO
☐   ☐

Name of creditor	Address (with postcode)	Amount owed to creditor £	What of yours is claimed and what is it worth?
1.			
2.			
3.			
4.			

Signature _____ Date _____

133

3b List of Unsecured Creditors

B

LIST OF UNSECURED CREDITORS

1 No.	2 Name of creditor or claimant	3 Address (with postcode)	4 Amount the creditor says you owe him/her £	5 Amount you think you owe £

Signature_____ Date_____

3ci Assets

C1

ASSETS

| | **Tick Box** | |
| | Yes | No |

Do you have any bank accounts or an interest in one?
If 'YES' state where they are, how much is in them and
how much is your share.

_____

_____

_____

_____

_____

Do you have any business bank accounts, including joint
accounts?
If 'YES' state the name of the accounts, where they are and
how much is in them.

_____

_____

_____

_____

Do you have any building society accounts or an interest in
one?
If 'YES' state where they are and how much is in them and
how much is your share.

_____

_____

_____

_____

_____

_____

Signature _____ **Date** _____

3cii Assets

C2

ASSETS

	Tick Box	
	Yes	No
Do you have any other savings? If **'YES'** give details	☐	☐

_____

_____

_____

_____

_____

	Yes	No
Do you use a motor vehicle? If **'YES'** who owns it and what is it worth?	☐	☐

_____

_____

_____

_____

	Yes	No
Have you an interest in any other motor vehicles? If **'YES'** give details and their value.	☐	☐

_____

_____

_____

_____

_____

_____

Signature _____ Date _____

3ciii Assets

C3

ASSETS

Now show anything else of yours which may be of value:	
	£
a) Household furniture and belongings_____	
b) Life policies_____	
c) Money owed to you_____	
d) Stock in trade_____	
e) Other property (see Guidance Notes)– _____	
	TOTAL

Signature _____ Date _____

3d

D

State the name, age (if under 18), and relationship to you of your dependants

1. _____ 6._____
2. _____ 7._____
3. _____ 8._____
4. _____ 9._____
5. _____ 10. _____

Has distress been levied against you by or on behalf of any creditor?
If **'YES'** give details below:

Tick Box

Yes   No
☐   ☐

Name of creditor	Amount of claim £	Date Distress levied	Description and estimated value of property seized
_____	_____	_____	_____
_____	_____	_____	_____
_____	_____	_____	_____
_____	_____	_____	_____
_____	_____	_____	_____
_____	_____	_____	_____
_____	_____	_____	_____
_____	_____	_____	_____
_____	_____	_____	_____
_____	_____	_____	_____
_____	_____	_____	_____

Signature _____   Date _____

3e

E

---

3. At the date you present your bankruptcy petition, is any court judgement or other legal process outstanding against you that has been made by any court in England and Wales?
If **'YES'** give details below:

Tick Box

Yes   No
☐   ☐

Name of creditor	Amount of claim £	Type and date of process issued	Description and estimated value of property involved
_____	_____	_____	_____
_____	_____	_____	_____
_____	_____	_____	_____
_____	_____	_____	_____
_____	_____	_____	_____
_____	_____	_____	_____
_____	_____	_____	_____
_____	_____	_____	_____
_____	_____	_____	_____

4. At the date you present your bankruptcy petition, is any attachment of earnings order in force against you?

If **'YES'** give details below:

Tick Box

Yes   No
☐   ☐

Name of creditor	Date of order	Court	Amount of instalment payable under order (per month/week)	Total amount paid under order	Date order expires (if applicable)
_____	_____	_____	£_____	£_____	_____
_____	_____	_____	_____	_____	_____
_____	_____	_____	_____	_____	_____
_____	_____	_____	_____	_____	_____

Signature _____   Date _____

3f

F

5(a) Have you, before you presented your petition, tried to come to any agreement with your creditors generally for payment of your debts?

Tick Box

Yes ☐   No ☐

(b) If the answer to 5(a) is **'YES'**, what terms were offered to the creditors:-

(1) Time for repayment_____

_____

(2) Total pence in £ receivable by creditors_____

_____

(3) When was the offer made?_____

_____

(c) Did the attempt fail because the creditors refused to accept the terms offered?

Tick Box

Yes ☐   No ☐

If **'NO'** why did it fail?_____

_____

_____

_____

6. Do you think that you will be able to introduce a voluntary arrangement to your creditors under Part VIII of Insolvency Act 1986, which is likely to be acceptable to them?

Tick Box

Yes ☐   No ☐

If **'YES'**, give brief details:

_____

_____

_____

_____

Signature_____   Date_____

140

3g Statement of Means

G

STATEMENT OF MEANS

(List below all items of regular 'monthly' income and expenditure)

Items of income	£	Items of expenditure	£	

This page shows that I will now be able to pay creditors £ _____ a month.

Signature _____   Date _____

4 Supplement to S.272 Debtor's Bankruptcy Petition Statement of Affairs

SUPPLEMENT TO S.272 DEBTOR'S BANKRUPTCY PETITION STATEMENT OF AFFAIRS

It will help the Court and speed up the hearing of your petition if you answer these questions correctly and in accordance with the details given by you in your Statement of Affairs.

	Tick correct box	
	Yes	**No**
1. Do you owe unsecured creditors❂ less than £20,000 in total? If NO, ignore questions 2 and 3.	☐	☐
2. Are your free assets† worth £2,000 or more?. If NO, ignore question 3.	☐	☐
3. Can you, as shown by page G of your Statement of Affairs, afford to make monthly payments to your creditors from your income?.	☐	☐

Signature: .... Date: ....

NOTES:

❂ UNSECURED CREDITORS are parties owed amounts which will not be paid off from the sale of property to which they have a prior claim (eg by a mortgage or charge on your home, life policies etc)

†FREE ASSETS are either:
(i) assets not claimed by creditors as security; or
(ii) the value of those assets shown on page A of your Statement of Affairs which you would receive if a secured creditor sold them to clear your debt and paid you the balance.

5 Claim Form

Claim Form

In the	
Claim No.	

Claimant(s)

SEAL

Defendant(s)

Amount of money claimed (where the claimant is making a claim for money)

Name and address of Defendant receiving this claim form

Amount claimed	
Court fee	
Solicitor's costs	
Total amount	
Issue date	

The Court office is open between 10 am and 4.30 pm Monday to Friday. When corresponding with the court, please address forms or letters to the Court Manager and quote the claim number.

N1(CC) - **w3** Claim form (CPR Part 7) (4.99)   *Printed on behalf of The Court Service*

Claim No.	

Brief details of claim

Particulars of claim (*attached)(*will follow if an acknowledgment of service is filed that indicates an intention to defend the claim)

Statement of Truth
*(I believe)(The Claimant believes) that the facts stated in this claim form *(and the particulars of the claim attached to this claim form) are true.
* I am duly authorised by the claimant to sign this statement
Full name _____

Name of *(claimant)(litigation friend's) (solicitor's firm)
_____

signed _____ position or office held _____
*(Claimant)(Litigation friend)('s solicitor)   (if signing on behalf of firm, company or corporation)
*delete as appropriate

Claimant's or litigation friend's or solicitor's address to which documents or payments should be sent if different from overleaf including (if appropriate) details of DX, fax or e-mail.

6 Application for an Administration Order (N92)

Application for an administration order

Please read the notes for guidance (form N270) before completing this form. Complete all details in black ink.

In the _____ **County Court**

Application Number _____ *For court use only*

Part A: statement of means

Please complete the following statement of means as fully as possible. Continue on a separate sheet if necessary.

1 Personal details

Full name

Full address

Mr ☐ Mrs ☐ Miss ☐ Ms ☐

Married ☐ Single ☐ Other *(specify)* ☐

Age

2 Dependants *(people you look after financially)*

Number of children in each age group

under 11 ☐ 11-15 ☐ 16-17 ☐ 18 & over ☐

Other dependants *(give details)*

3 Bank/Building society accounts and savings

☐ I have a current account

☐ The account is in **credit** by £

☐ The account is **overdrawn** by £

☐ I have a savings or deposit account

☐ The amount in the account is £

I have other savings or investments

(give details)

4 Employment

Complete all the boxes that apply. If you are not in paid employment and are not seeking work eg a homemaker, you should say so in the unemployment section.

☐ I am employed as a

My employer *(include address)*

My works number and/or pay reference

Jobs other than main job *(give details)*

☐ I have been unemployed for *(say how long)*

Do you have any reason to believe that you may be able to obtain employment within the next three months?

☐ I am self employed as a

Give details of:
(a) contracts and other work in hand

(b) any sums due for work done £

☐ I receive a pension

5 Property

I live in

☐ my own property

☐ jointly owned property

☐ rented property

☐ lodgings

☐ other eg with parents

£ _____ amount due under a mortgage/ charges against property

£ _____ value of property

N92 - w3 Application for an Administration Order (Order 35, rule 2(1))(2.99)

Statement of means - income and expenditure

♦ Important: It will help the court if you give all sums for income and expenditure as either monthly or weekly figures. Try not to mix the two.

6. Income

See page 2 of the notes for guidance before completing this section

specify weekly/monthly

			specify weekly/monthly	
My usual take home pay	£	Sub total brought forward	£
My partner contributes to the expenses listed in section 7	£	Income support *(see notes for guidance)*	£
Others living in my home give me	£	Child benefit(s)	£
My pension(s)	£	Other state benefits *(specify)*	
Other income *(give details)*			£
	£		£
Sub total	£	Total	£

7. Regular expenses and arrears

See page 3 of the notes for guidance before completing any part of this section

	(a) Regular payments Enter the amount you usually spend or must pay for each item, weekly or monthly *(please complete each entry: write n/a if not applicable)*	**(b) Total arrears** If you are in arrears with any of the items in the regular payments column(a), enter the total arrears owed in column (b). Full details should be given in the list of creditors *(see notes for guidance)*.	**(c) Regular arrears payments** If you are paying off the arrears shown in column (b) show much you are paying weekly or monthly in column (c). Do not include these amounts as regular payments in column (a).
	weekly/monthly		*weekly/monthly*
Rent	£	£	£
Mortgage/home loan	£	£	£
Second mortgage/secured loan	£	£	£
Life insurance/endowment	£	£	£
House contents insurance	£	£	£
Council tax/community charge arrears	£	£	£
Maintenance/child support	£	£	£
Water/sewerage charges	£	£	£
Groundrent/service charge	£	£	£
Gas (or other fuel eg coal, oil)	£	£	£
Electricity	£	£	£
TV rental / licence	£	£	£
Magistrates' Court fine(s)	£	£	£
DSS Social Fund Loan/overpaid benefit	£	£	£
Telephone *(line, phone rental essential calls only)*	£	£	£
Child care	£	£	£
Food and household essentials	£	£	£
Clothing	£	£	£
Laundry	£	£	£
Travelling expenses *(essential eg work, school)*	£	£	£
School meals/meals at work	£	£	£
Prescriptions/dentists/optician	£	£	£
Others *(eg hire purchase)* *(see notes for guidance)*			
	£	£	£
	£	£	£
	£	£	£

7a Total expenses

£	per w/m

7b Total arrears

£

Part B: list of creditors *(see page 4 of the notes for guidance)*

Applicant's name	Application Number *For court use only*	

Name of creditor, if known, and address to which payment should be sent. Give reference/account number. If judgment debt, also state court and case number *(see example 3 in notes for guidance).*	If someone else is jointly responsible for part of this debt give details (eg guarantor, joint account etc)	Amount outstanding	
		£	p
		Sub total		

List of creditors - continued

Name of creditor, if known, and address to which payment should be sent. Give reference/account number. If judgment debt, also state court and case number.	If someone else is jointly responsible for part of this debt give details (eg guarantor, joint account etc)	Amount outstanding	
		£	p
	Sub total brought forward		
	Total		

continue on a separate sheet if necessary

Part C: offer of payment

You do not have to make an offer of payment as the court will fix a rate for you to pay based on the information you have given on this form. If you do make an offer, it should be one you can afford to pay.

I offer to pay by instalments of £ _____ per week/month

[ ] **Please tick if you object to the court making an attachment of earnings order and give your reasons in the space opposite** *(see notes for guidance).*

If you wish the court to take anything else into account when making an order, please give details *(see notes for guidance).*

Part D: declaration

(to be signed and sworn or affirmed before an officer of the court)

Before you sign this form take it to the court office with a copy of the judgment or order *(see notes for guidance)*

I ask the court to make an administration order.

I _____ (full name)

of _____ (address)

declare on oath/affirm that to the best of my knowledge, the names of all creditors, and the debts I owe them, are truly recorded in the list of creditors and that the information I have given in my application and the statement of means is true.

_____ Signature

Sworn/affirmed at:

in the County of _____ this _____ day of _____ 19 ____

before me

Officer of the court, appointed by the Judge to take affidavits pursuant to s.58 of the County Courts Act 1984

148

7 Application for Suspension of a Warrant and/or Variation of an Order (N245)

<table>
<tr>
<td colspan="2">

Application for suspension of a warrant and/or variation of an order

- *Read these notes carefully before completing the form.*
- *Tick the correct boxes and give as much information as you can. It will help the court make a fair decision about how much you can afford to pay if the plaintiff refuses your offer.*
- *If you do not complete all the details and sign the form, the court will not be able to deal with your application.*
- *The court will send you an order giving details of how and when to pay or will tell you when to come to court. You will be informed of the court's decision.*
- *You will have to pay a fee for your application. You can get details of the fee to pay and information about what to do if you cannot pay all or part of a fee from any county court office*

</td>
<td>

In the

              Court

Claim Number

Warrant No.	**Local No.**

Claimant *(including ref.)*

Defendant

For court use only	**Date copy sent to claimant**	

</td>
</tr>
</table>

I cannot pay the amount ordered and

I wish to apply for

☐ suspension of the warrant

and/or

☐ a reduction in the instalment order

1 Personal details

Surname

Forename

☐ Mr ☐ Mrs ☐ Miss ☐ Ms

☐ Married ☐ Single ☐ Other *(specify)*

Age

Address

Postcode

2 Dependants *(people you look after financially)*

Children *(under 19)*		Others *(give details)*
Age	Date of Birth	

(If more continue on a separate sheet)

3 Employment

☐ I am employed as a

My employer is

Jobs other than main job *(give details)*

☐ I am self employed as a

Annual turnover is £

☐ **I am not** in arrears with my national insurance contributions, income tax and VAT

☐ **I am** in arrears and I owe £

Give details of:
(a) contracts and other work in hand
(b) any sums due for work done

☐ I have been unemployed for _____ years _____ months

☐ I am a pensioner

4 Bank account and savings

☐ I have a bank account

    ☐ The account is in credit by £

    ☐ The account is overdrawn by £

☐ I have a savings account or building society account

    The amount in the account is £

5 Property

I live in ☐ my own property ☐ lodgings

    ☐ jointly owned property ☐ council property

    ☐ rented property

N245 - w3 - Form for applying for suspension of warrant of execution or reduction of instalment order (4.99) *Printed on behalf of The Court Service*

Managing Debt

6 Income

My usual take home pay *(including overtime, commission, bonuses etc.)*	£	per
Income support	£	per
Child benefit(s)	£	per
Other state benefit(s)	£	per
My pension(s)	£	per
Others living in my home give me	£	per
Other income *(give details below)*		
	£	per
	£	per
	£	per
Total income	£	per

8 Priority debts

(This section is for arrears only. Do not include regular expenses listed in box 7)

Rent arrears		£	per
Mortgage arrears		£	per
Council tax arrears		£	per
Water charge arrears		£	per
Fuel debts:	Gas	£	per
	Electricity	£	per
	Other	£	per
Maintenance arrears		£	per
Others *(give details below)*			
		£	per
		£	per
Total priority debts		£	per

7 Expenses

(Do not include any payments made by other members of the household out of their own income)

I have regular expenses as follows:

Mortgage *(including second mortgage)*	£	per
Rent	£	per
Council tax	£	per
Gas	£	per
Electricity	£	per
Water charges	£	per
TV rental and licence	£	per
HP repayments	£	per
Mail order	£	per
Housekeeping, food, school meals	£	per
Travelling expenses	£	per
Childrenís clothing	£	per
Maintenance payments	£	per
Others *(not court orders or credit debts listed in boxes 9 and 10)*		
	£	per
	£	per
	£	per
Total expenses	£	per

9 Court orders

Court	Claim No.	£	per

Total court order instalments	£	per

Of the payments above, I am behind with payments to *(please list)*

10 Credit debts

Loans and credit card debts *(please list)*

	£	per
	£	per
	£	per

Of the payments above, I am behind with payments to *(please list)*

11 Offer of Payment

- *If you take away the totals of boxes 7, 8 and 9 and the payments you are making in box 10 from the total in box 6, you will get some idea of the sort of sum you should offer. The offer you make should be one you can afford.*

I can pay	£	a month
(and I enclose	£	)
I also enclose the fee of	£	

12 Declaration

I declare that the details I have given above are true to the best of my knowledge

Signed		Date	

150

8 Application Notice (N244)

Application Notice

- You must complete Parts A **and** B, **and** Part C if applicable
- Send any relevant fee and the completed application notice to the court with any draft order, witness statement or other evidence
- It is for you (and not the court) to serve this application notice

In the	
Claim No.	
Warrant no. (if applicable)	
Claimant(s) (including ref.)	
Defendant(s) (including ref.)	
Date	

You should provide this information for listing the application

Time estimate   (hours)   (mins)

Is this agreed by all parties?   Yes ☐   No ☐

Please always refer to the Commercial Court Guide for details of how applications should be prepared and will be heard, or in a small number of exceptional cases can be dealt with on paper.

Part A

1. Where there is more than one claimant or defendant, specify which claimant or defendant

(The claimant)(The defendant)[1]

2. State clearly what order you are seeking (if there is room) or otherwise refer to a draft order (which must be attached)

intend(s) to apply for an order (a draft of which is attached) that[2]

3. Briefly set out why you are seeking the order. Identify any rule or statutory provision

because[3]

The court office is open from 10am to 4.30 pm Monday to Friday. When corresponding with the court please address forms or letters to the Clerk to the Commercial Court and quote the claim number.

N244 (CC) - w3 Application Notice (4.99)   *Printed on behalf of The Court Service*

Part B

(The claimant)(The defendant)[1] wishes to rely on: *tick one:*

the attached (witness statement)(affidavit) ☐   (the claimant)(the defendant)'s[1] statement of case ☐

evidence in Part C overleaf in support of this application ☐

Signed		**Position or office held** (if signing on behalf of firm, company or corporation)	
	(Applicant)('s litigation friend) ('s solicitor)		

4. If you are not already a party to the proceedings, you must provide an address for service of documents

Address to which documents about this claim should be sent (including reference if appropriate)[4]

		if applicable	
	Tel. no.		
	fax no.		
	DX no.		
Postcode	e-mail		

Part C

Claim No. [   ]

(Note: Part C should only be used where it is convenient to enter here the evidence in support of the application, rather than to use witness statements or affidavits)

(The claimant)(The defendant)[1] wishes to rely on the following evidence in support of this application:

Statement of Truth

*(I believe)(The applicant believes) that the facts stated in this application notice are true

*I am duly authorised by the applicant to sign this statement

Full name...

Name of*(Applicant)('s litigation friend)('s solicitor)

....

Signed [   ]

*(Applicant)('s litigation friend)('s solicitor)

Position or office held [   ]
(if signing on behalf of firm, company or corporation)

*delete as appropriate

Date [   ]

Glossary

Administration Order If you have at least one County or High Court Judgment against you, then you can make an application for an Administration Order, which is an arrangement under which the Court will administer the repayment of your debts to your creditors. The main conditions are that you must have at least two debts and the total of all your debts must not exceed £5,000. In this arrangement, you make one monthly payment to the Court, which will distribute it between your creditors, pro rata according to the amount owed to each.

Affidavit A sworn statement which is signed by the debtor.

Annual Percentage Rate (APR) APR measures the rate of total charge for credit. It includes not only interest but also administrative charges, documentation fees and maintenance charges. The APR must be included in all advertisements for credit and in agreements regulated by the Consumer Credit Act 1974.

Attachment of Earnings Order If you are employed, or receive an occupational pension, and a Judgment has been made against you which you have defaulted on, a creditor can ask the Court to order that the debt should be paid directly to them from your earnings or pension. In order to do this a creditor will apply to the Court which will send you a form asking for details of your income and expenditure. This form must be returned to the Court within eight days. Once an order is made, your employer has to make the payments to your creditor under an Attachment of Earnings Order.

Attendance Allowance This is the non-contributory, non-means-tested and non-taxable social security benefit for the care needs of people over the age of 65.

Bailiffs The main function of a bailiff is the collection of debt. The means of enforcement used by bailiffs is to seize and sell goods to pay off a debt. There are two main types of bailiff:

- County Court bailiffs – employees of the County Court, they enforce County Court Judgments, for example for consumer credit debts.
- Private bailiffs – employees of private companies used by the Magistrates Courts to collect fines, and by local authorities (after the award of a Liability Order from the Magistrates Court) to collect Council Tax.

Bankruptcy If you are insolvent (ie unable to pay your debts because your liabilities are greater than your assets), you may wish to consider bankruptcy. You should not do this without advice as there may be alternatives (eg an IVA – see below). Bankruptcy is formal legal recognition of your insolvency. In a bankruptcy an Official Receiver or a Trustee in bankruptcy will be appointed by the Court to take over the handling of your financial affairs. They will administer your affairs in the interests of your creditors.

Charging Order This is a way of enforcing a County Court Judgment, by making the debt into a secured debt. This means that the debt becomes charged on your property – like a mortgage.

Claim This is the Court document which has to be served on you to initiate an action to recover money. It will include details (particulars) of the claim and will explain how and when you should respond.

Committal hearings These are hearings in the Magistrates Court, normally regarding non-payment of a Magistrates Court fine or in respect of Council Tax.

Compensation Order This is an order which a criminal Court can make against a convicted person. It orders them to pay a specified sum to the victim of the crime.

Composition Order This is the term for a Court order which a judge can make where you can demonstrate that you cannot clear your debts in a reasonable time (eg three years). The judge can make an order that you are only required to pay a specified proportion of your total debts and the rest will be written off.

Consumer Credit Act (CCA) The Consumer Credit Act 1974 is the main piece of legislation governing the giving of credit. Its provisions include: the definition of APR; the licensing of credit lenders and debt collection; the regulation of credit agreements; and the rules on extortionate credit.

Council Tax This is the local government tax payable by individuals. It has to be treated as a priority debt because of the potential for the imposition of a *Liability Order* (see below) and the ultimate threat of imprisonment for wilful non-payment.

County Court This is the main Court which deals with civil debt cases. In general Court staff deal with administrative issues and undisputed cases. District and circuit judges deal with disputed cases.

Credit reference file A record of your credit history, held by Credit Reference Agencies. The file keeps information, both good and bad, about any credit accounts you have. It will show whether payments are made on time or not. It also keeps details of any County Court Judgments and whether you are on the electoral role. Creditors may look at the information on your file to decide whether to give you credit.

Credit unions Credit unions are organisations run either in a local community or a workplace. Each credit union is run by its own members and encourages regular saving and offers loan facilities.

Default Notice If a credit agreement is regulated by the Consumer Credit Act, your creditor must normally serve a Default Notice before they can start Court proceedings against you. This terminates the agreement if the default goes uncorrected. It is a demand for immediate repayment of the debt and all other money due (ie interest, charges etc) although it can be just for the arrears. A Default Notice has to be in a particular form laid down by regulations and it must tell you how you can make good the breach of the agreement.

Disability Living Allowance This is a non-contributory, non-means-tested social security benefit for the care and mobility needs of disabled people under the age of 65.

Distress Warrant 'Distress' is the process of recovering debts by using a bailiff to take goods which belong to the debtor. A warrant is written permission – usually from a Court for the bailiff to attempt to take goods.

Equity The equity in a home is the value left after deduction of any current securities such as a mortgage and/or second mortgage.

Execution (see *Warrant of Execution*)

Full and final settlement A payment (usually a lump sum) made to a creditor which is less than the total amount owed – however, in return for receiving the lump sum the creditor agrees to write off the rest of the debt.

Garnishee Order This is an Order that allows one of your creditors to force someone who 'owes' you money or holds your money (ie your bank) to pay it direct to that creditor.

High Court The High Court is the superior civil Court in England and Wales. Court actions for debt should only be started in the High Court where the debt is more than £15,000 and involves complex issues.

Hire Purchase (HP) In a Hire Purchase agreement, goods are hired to you by the lender until the final instalment of the loan is paid. At that point in time you may exercise an option to purchase the goods. Alternatively you can return the goods to the owner.

Housing Benefit This is the means-tested social security benefit that helps with the cost of paying rent if you are a tenant. There are detailed qualifying conditions.

Income Support (Minimum Income Guarantee) This is the main means-tested social security benefit. There are detailed qualifying conditions.

Individual Voluntary Arrangement (IVA) An IVA is a formal way of making an arrangement with your creditors that avoids bankruptcy. To be able to apply for an IVA you have to be able to either raise a lump sum and/or make a regular payment.

Instalment Order If you have replied to a Court summons by admitting the debt, and asking for time to pay, the Court will be likely to make an Instalment Order, setting out the amounts you need to pay to the creditor.

Judgment This is the legal term for a Court order which has been made against you in the action which has been brought by your creditor. It allows the creditor to take enforcement action against you to recover the debt if you default.

Jurisdiction There are detailed rules about the venue of the court, and the type of court, which your creditor must use to pursue a claim against you.

Liability Order The Magistrates Court can issue a Liability Order for Council Tax, Community Charge and business rates arrears, at the request of a local authority. A Liability Order allows the local authority to take enforcement action against you to recover the debt.

Magistrates Court The Magistrates Court is a criminal Court but also deals with Liability Orders for Council Tax, Community Charge and business rates. It also holds committal hearings for these debts.

Minimum Income Guarantee (see *Income Support*)

Non-priority debts These are those debts, such as consumer debts, which cannot be treated as a priority. This does not mean that they can be ignored but rather that they need to be looked at *after* you have reached agreement with your priority creditors as they usually incur less severe penalties for non-payment.

Official Receiver This is the title for the official who administers bankruptcies in England and Wales.

Personal Budget A sheet which has all of a debtor's income and expenditure on it, showing what is owed, to whom, and details of what surplus income is available.

Possession proceedings This is the type of Court action that will be raised against you if you have a mortgage or a secured loan and you have defaulted on it. It can lead to you losing your home.

Priority debts This term is used to describe those debts which you have to take most seriously because of the serious consequences of non-payment due to the powers of the creditor. These debts have to be dealt with before non-priority debts from any disposable income. Examples include mortgage arrears (risk of loss of your home) and Council Tax (risk of imprisonment).

Protected Earnings Rate If a creditor applies to the County Court to make an Attachment of Earnings Order against you, the Court will look at whether your salary or pension is below a certain level, called the *Protected Earnings Rate*. If it is below this level, then an attachment will not be made.

Refinancing This is the term used to describe the process of restructuring your finances. This could involve, for example, taking on a consolidating loan as a means of reducing your weekly or monthly repayments. If you are thinking of doing this you should get advice from an independent financial adviser.

Regulated agreements A regulated agreement is one which is governed by the Consumer Credit Act 1974. This is defined as *'an agreement by which the creditor provides the individual with credit not exceeding £25,000'* unless it is specifically exempt.

Rescheduling This is the term for agreeing with your existing creditors that they will accept revised repayments (ie that they will not hold you to the original contractual repayments). It may involve lengthening the period of repayments. If possible, you should try to have interest frozen for a period to avoid increasing the amount repaid as much as possible.

Secured loan If you have granted a charge over your home as security for a loan and you default on the loan, you may put your home at risk as the creditor may begin steps to recover the house from you.

Small Claims A disputed debt of less than £5,000 will normally be dealt with under the Small Claims Track unless particularly complicated issues of law are involved.

Social Fund loan A Social Fund loan may be either a crisis loan or a budgeting loan. A budgeting loan is a loan from the Benefits Agency. You must have been receiving Income Support or income-based Jobseeker's Allowance for 26 weeks. The loan is usually for items that are difficult to budget for. How much you can borrow will depend on how long you have been on benefit and who is in your household. A crisis loan is to meet expenses which arise in an emergency. You do not have to be in receipt of benefit to apply for this loan, but certain items of expenditure (such as Court fees) cannot be covered by a crisis loan.

Time Order This is an Order made only in respect of agreements regulated by the Consumer Credit Act 1974. On an application by you, the County Court can change certain aspects of a credit agreement, including the interest rate and how long the loan will last.

Voluntary Charge This is an arrangement whereby you give a non-priority creditor security over your home as part of a settlement of your debt problem. You should think very carefully before doing this and seek advice.

Walking Possession Order If a bailiff is let into your property when trying to enforce a debt, they may choose not to take any goods with them. Instead they may make a list of goods (an 'inventory') which they will then ask you to sign. This is called a Walking Possession Order and it means that you cannot remove the goods – the bailiff can come back at a later date and take the goods if the debt has still not been paid.

Warrant of Execution If payments are not made under a County Court Judgment, the creditor can apply for a Warrant of Execution. This gives the County Court bailiffs the power to try to collect payment on behalf of the creditor by calling at your home and trying to either obtain payment or take goods (or list the goods and leave them there) to the value of the amount on the warrant.

Warrant for Possession This grants County Court bailiffs the power to evict the occupiers of a house and to change the locks.

Write off A write off is where a creditor or creditors will agree not to pursue the debtor further for the sums owed (or part) and they accept that the debt is unrecoverable.

Useful addresses

The national organisations listed below may be able to help or put you in touch with a local source of advice.

Age Concern England
1268 London Road
London SW16 4ER
Tel: 020 8765 7200
Age Concern Information Line 0800 00 99 66
Website: www.ageconcern.org.uk
Can put you in touch with your local Age Concern.

Association of British Credit Unions Ltd (ABCUL)
Holyoake House
Hanover Street
Manchester M60 0AS
Tel: 0161 832 3694
Website: www.abcul.org
Will be able to tell you if there is a credit union in your area.

Association of Charity Officers (incorporating the Occupational Benevolent Funds Alliance)
Beechwood House
Wyllyotts Close
Potters Bar
Hertfordshire EN6 2HW
Tel: 01707 651777
Provides information about charities that make grants to individuals in need.

Bankruptcy Association of Great Britain and Ireland
4 Johnson Close
Abraham Heights
Lancaster LA1 5EU
Tel: 01524 64305
Provides advice to people facing bankruptcy.

Birmingham Settlement
318 Summer Lane
Newtown
Birmingham B19 3RL
Tel: 0121 248 3000
National Debtline: 0808 808 4000
Runs National Debtline and offers free information pack on dealing with debt.

Carers UK
20-25 Glasshouse Yard
London EC1A 4JT
Tel: 020 7490 8818
Helpline: 0808 808 7777 (weekdays 10am-12pm and 2pm-4pm)
Provides general advice and help for all carers.

Charity Search
25 Portview Road
Avonmouth
Bristol BS11 9LD
Tel: 0117 982 4060, weekdays 10am-4pm
Helps link older people with charities that may provide grants to individuals. Applications in writing are preferred.

Council of Mortgage Lenders
3 Savile Row
London W1X 1AF
Tel: 020 7440 2255
Website: www.cml.org.uk
Association representing mortgage lenders. Only recorded information available.

Energywatch
Tel: 0800 88 77 77
Gas complaints: 0845 906 0708
Electricity complaints: 0845 601 3131
Website: www.energywatch.org.uk
New independent consumer organisation representing the interests of all gas and electricity consumers.

Financial Services Authority
25 The North Colonnade
Canary Wharf
London E14 5HS
Public Enquiries Office: 0845 606 1234
Website: www.fsa.gov.uk
Regulates the financial services industry and provides information to consumers.

IFA Promotion Ltd
6th Floor
117 Farringdon Road
London EC1R 3BX
Tel: 020 7833 3131
Hotline: 0117 971 1177
Phone their hotline for a list of independent financial advisers in your area. They also publish a free booklet on choosing an independent financial adviser.

Insolvency Service
Tel: 020 7291 6895 (9am-5pm, weekdays)
Website: www.insolvency.gov.uk
The Insolvency Service is an Executive Agency of the Department for Trade and Industry.

Institute of Chartered Accountants
Chartered Accountants' Hall
PO Box 433
Moorgate Place
London EC2P 2BJ
Tel: 020 7920 8100
Website: www.icaew.co.uk/
Recognised professional body which can help you find a local firm of accountants.

Law Centres Federation
Duchess House
18-19 Warren Street
London W1T 5LR
Tel: 020 7387 8570
Website: www.lawcentres.org.uk
Can tell you if there is a law centre in your area.

Money Advice Association
Kempton House
Dysart Road
Grantham
Lincolnshire NG31 7LE
Tel: 01476 594970
Website: www.m-a-a.org.uk
The umbrella organisation for money advice providers for England and Wales.

National Insurance Contributions Office (NICO)
Benton Park Road
Longbenton
Newcastle Upon Tyne NE98 1YX
Website: www.inlandrevenue.gov.uk
Deals with NI contributions records and payments.

Office of Fair Trading (OFT)
Tel: 0870 606 0321
Website: www.oft.gov.uk
Has a leaflet called Don't Let Credit Turn into Debt, *an APR ready reckoner and a budget calculator (you may also be able to get these from your local CAB or Trading Standards Office). Ran the 'Keep Debt Under Control' Campaign with the Trading Standards Institute.*

OFGEM
9 Millbank
London SW1P 3GE
Tel: 020 7901 7000
Website: www.ofgem.gov.uk
The regulatory body for fuel supplies.

Office of Water Services (OFWAT)
7 Hill Street
Birmingham
B5 4UA
Tel: 0121 625 1300
Website: www.ofwat.gov.uk
The regulatory body for the water industry.

Shelter
88 Old Street
London EC1V 9HU
Tel: 020 7505 4699
Shelterline (24-hour): Freephone 0808 800 4444
Website: www.shelter.org.uk
National homelessness charity which can offer advice to those facing repossession or eviction.

About Age Concern

Managing debt is one of a wide range of publications produced by Age Concern England, the National Council on Ageing. Age Concern works on behalf of all older people and believes later life should be fulfilling and enjoyable. For too many this is impossible. As the leading charitable movement in the UK concerned with ageing and older people, Age Concern finds effective ways to change that situation.

Where possible, we enable older people to solve problems themselves, providing as much or as little support as they need. A network of local Age Concerns, supported by 250,000 volunteers, provides community-based services such as lunch clubs, day centres and home visiting.

Nationally, we take a lead role in campaigning, parliamentary work, policy analysis, research, specialist information and advice provision, and publishing. Innovative programmes promote healthier lifestyles and provide older people with opportunities to give the experience of a lifetime back to their communities.

Age Concern is dependent on donations, covenants and legacies.

Age Concern England
1268 London Road
London SW16 4ER
Tel: 020 8765 7200
Fax: 020 8765 7211

Age Concern Cymru
4th Floor
1 Cathedral Road
Cardiff CF1 9SD
Tel: 029 2037 1566
Fax: 029 2039 9562

Age Concern Scotland
113 Rose Street
Edinburgh EH2 3DT
Tel: 0131 220 3345
Fax: 0131 220 2779

Age Concern Northern Ireland
3 Lower Crescent
Belfast BT7 1NR
Tel: 028 9024 5729
Fax: 028 9023 5497

Publications from Age Concern Books

Your Rights: A guide to money benefits for older people

Sally West

A highly successful, popular book, *Your Rights* ensures that older people – and their advisers – can easily understand the complexities of State benefits. Updated annually, and written in jargon-free language, it has helped more than 2.7 million people discover the full range of benefits available to them.

Using Your Home as Capital

Cecil Hinton and David McGrath

This best-selling book for homeowners is updated annually and gives a detailed explanation of how to capitalise on the value of your home and obtain a regular additional income.

Please contact Age Concern Books at the address below for more information.

If you would like to order any of these titles, please write to the address below, enclosing a cheque or money order for the appropriate amount (plus £1.95 p&p) made payable to Age Concern England. Credit card orders may be made on 0870 44 22 044 (individuals) or 0870 44 22 120 (AC federation, other organisations and institutions).

Age Concern Books
PO Box 232
Newton Abbot
Devon TQ12 4XQ

Age Concern Information Line/Factsheets subscription

Age Concern produces 44 comprehensive factsheets designed to answer many of the questions older people (or those advising them) may have. These include money and benefits, health, community care, leisure and education, and housing. For up to five free factsheets, telephone: 0800 00 99 66 (7am-7pm, seven days a week, every day of the year). Alternatively you may prefer to write to Age Concern, FREEPOST (SWB 30375), Ashburton, Devon TQ13 7ZZ.

For professionals working with older people, the factsheets are available on an annual subscription service, which includes updates throughout the year. For further details and costs of the subscription, please write to Age Concern at the above Freepost address.

Index